MW00413932

PRAISE FOR IRON AND COTTON

What if every future husband had a wise, informed, fun, encouraging friend to help prep them for marriage? Now they do. In Iron and Cotton, Mike not only gives you tools, but he also shows you how to use them. Future husbands, already husbands, read this. I promise you will be glad you did.

TED LOWE, AUTHOR OF *YOUR BEST US*

The best authors are often the ones with the most passion for their subject. Mike's passion for preparing and ultimately guiding young men through marriage shines clearly in "Iron and Cotton." Using a casual, everyman tone, he brings to life the challenges and joys of marriage in a quick, enjoyable, and insightful read.

DAVID PURDUM, ESPN WRITER

Mike's original goal is one we all share – equipping our sons and future sons-in-law with the tools and principles to be great husbands! This practical book will be valuable to men who aspire to marry and even to those who are already married.

PETER BOURKE, AUTHOR, *MEN YOUR MARRIAGE MATTERS TO GOD*

"Iron and Cotton is a breath of fresh air for anyone who wants to grow in their faith and in their marriage. Mike masterfully weaves inspiration and practical application onto every page. I highly recommend this book."

DAVE WILLIS, AUTHOR, PASTOR, AND CO-HOST OF THE NAKED MARRIAGE PODCAST

Iron and Cotton addresses virtually every issue we encounter and teach as marriage counselors of fifteen years. It's a wonderful "field guide" for the young, soon-to-be-married guys, but I believe every husband should read it periodically to keep his marriage thriving and growing.

GARY DELAPLANE, MOURNING DOVE COUNSELING

"I hope that men out there are able to understand and value the amount of knowledge and wisdom that is shared in this book. Mike writes from a refreshing perspective on a topic I feel as though men often don't honestly talk about. It has impacted me and my relationship with my wife. I hope it does the same for you."

TIMOTHY WENGER - THEMANEFFECT.COM

"Mike's field manual is an essential read for anyone either currently married or considering marriage! His direct, plain-spoken language conveying his insight on making marriage thrive makes Iron and Cotton a book I highly endorse!"

JUSTIN BAILEY - CODE OF CHARACTER, CODEOFCHARACTER.COM

"This book should be in the hands of all men that desire to build emotional intimacy with their partner. It is easy to read, relatable to men young and old, and targets an often neglected part of communication - asking questions! The author gives fantastic examples of how to take a common conversation and turn it into meaningful dialogue."

KERRY JO SCHNEIDER, MS, LPC

IRON & COTTON:

A Man's Field Guide to Marriage

MIKE POVENZ

© Mike Povenz 2021

ISBN: 978-1-09838-871-3
eBook ISBN: 978-1-09838-872-0

Editor: Josh Raab

CONTENTS

Dear⎯⎯⎯⎯⎯⎯⎯⎯⎯⎯⎯⎯⎯⎯⎯⎯⎯⎯

⎯⎯⎯⎯⎯⎯⎯⎯⎯⎯⎯⎯⎯⎯⎯⎯⎯⎯⎯⎯⎯⎯⎯⎯⎯⎯⎯⎯⎯⎯

⎯⎯⎯⎯⎯⎯⎯⎯⎯⎯⎯⎯⎯⎯⎯⎯⎯⎯⎯⎯⎯⎯⎯⎯⎯⎯⎯⎯⎯⎯

⎯⎯⎯⎯⎯⎯⎯⎯⎯⎯⎯⎯⎯⎯⎯⎯⎯⎯⎯⎯⎯⎯⎯⎯⎯⎯⎯⎯⎯⎯

⎯⎯⎯⎯⎯⎯⎯⎯⎯⎯⎯⎯⎯⎯⎯⎯⎯⎯⎯⎯⎯⎯⎯⎯⎯⎯⎯⎯⎯⎯

⎯⎯⎯⎯⎯⎯⎯⎯⎯⎯⎯⎯⎯⎯⎯⎯⎯⎯⎯⎯⎯⎯⎯⎯⎯⎯⎯⎯⎯⎯

⎯⎯⎯⎯⎯⎯⎯⎯⎯⎯⎯⎯⎯⎯⎯⎯⎯⎯⎯⎯⎯⎯⎯⎯⎯⎯⎯⎯⎯⎯

With love,

⎯⎯⎯⎯⎯⎯⎯⎯⎯⎯⎯⎯⎯⎯⎯⎯⎯⎯⎯⎯

DEDICATION

To my wife Brandy:

You have given me the greatest adventure a man can ask for. Marrying my best friend was the best decision I ever made. Thank you for being by my side and allowing me to be by yours for twenty years. Life is so much richer and fuller with you in it. You are a continual inspiration to me and a beacon of light in my life and the lives of so many others. I am so proudly tethered to you in our marriage, a bond I see as a lifeline and jump rope of fun for us both. Your love and respect for me give me the confidence to take on the world. I am forever grateful to you. Thank you for your incredible patience and support as I wrote this book. Whatever life offers us next, I fear nothing with you by my side.

To my son Lachlan: I wrote this for you, tough guy.

To my daughters Lily and Breckyn: I wrote this because of you.

And to my future sons-in-law: Take notes; I have a quiz for you at the end.

DISCLAIMER

ABUSE IS NOT LOVE; it never has been and never will be. The abuse you may have experienced or witnessed was not okay. Healing from these events and pursuing recovery should be at the top of your list. Nobody should be in an abusive relationship. Nobody.

Verbal abuse is a communication style that is unhealthy and unwanted. Verbal abuse *is* abuse. Seek change or counseling immediately if you are insulting, constantly criticizing, name-calling, threatening, blaming, accusing, and humiliating your partner. Seek help if this is happening to you.

Visit the following website for more information:

https://www.thehotline.org/resources/types-of-abuse/

ABOUT MIKE POVENZ

MIKE POVENZ HAS A passion for helping men discover the best version of themselves and for guiding them to be better husbands and fathers. He is the founder of Modern Chivalry Men, an organization that inspires men to positive change and community involvement. He is also the host of *Iron and Cotton*, a podcast. Mike has served for years as a men's group leader and is the recipient of the *Life Changer Award*. He lives in North Georgia with his beloved wife of twenty years. They are the proud parents of three children, Lily, Lachlan, and Breckyn, along with three dogs, two guinea pigs, four chickens, and one psychotic fish. Mike loves the outdoors, fishing, boating, skiing, cooking on cast iron, and time with family and friends.

ABOUT IRON AND COTTON

IRON AND COTTON IS an organization focused on inspiring men to be full of character, strength, and compassion.

Iron and Cotton is a bold way of life for the modern-day man—a man who seeks wisdom from the past and shields himself from societal norms that aim to corrupt his future. Courageously, he allows himself to be forged like iron into something stronger, sharper, and more useful. Fearlessly, he seeks to interweave into himself a common thread of decency, care, and understanding. He can often be found carrying a pocketknife and handkerchief as symbolic tools to remind him of his mission to offer his strength and compassion to all in his path. Strength and compassion are evident in his actions, not just his words. He finds adventure in his intentional and purposeful quest to become a better man, husband, and father. He inspires other men through his authenticity and not his prideful pursuits.

Follow and learn more at www.ironandcotton.org; #ironandcotton, podcast; "Iron and Cotton."; www.modernchivalrymen.org; and #modernchivalrymen

PREFACE

I WROTE THIS BOOK FOR men who want to enter marriage with their eyes wide open and their hearts prepared for life's greatest and most rewarding journey.

If you're anything like me, you weren't searching for this book; someone gifted it to you. If that's the case, I would ask you to honor this gift and appreciate it. Someone wants the best for you and your relationship, and they are investing in you, your future, and your potential. This is not a judgment on you and your abilities as a man and husband; it's a desire for you to have the best life.

Whether you sought this book out on your own or were gifted it and dared to open it up: bravo, brothers. You are off to an incredible start. You are already defying the odds and investing early in your marriage. You have taken the massive step of realizing there is more to know and information to be gathered.

INTRODUCTION

Life is a journey, and if you fall in love with the journey, you will be in love forever. – Peter Hagerty

When setting out on a journey, do not seek advice from someone who never left home. – Rumi

Focus on the journey, not the destination. Joy is found not in finishing an activity but in doing it. – Greg Anderson

---

CHEERS ERUPT AS THE bride and groom kiss and are announced husband and wife. Encircled by loved ones and a beautiful autumn day, they begin their stroll off the platform and down to a rustic barn. A charming and finely decorated outdoor wedding is well underway, and memories are being made with every passing second.

Five years later, this once vibrant couple partakes in another significant event: a cold, vacant, and draining day of divorce court. Two people who were once embraced in pure love and excitement now sit far from each other silently and only speak through lawyers.

How could this happen? How did this couple grow so distant from each other? Where did they go wrong? And how about those couples who do not divorce but find themselves trapped in a loveless and sexless marriage? How does that happen?

In the pages ahead, we will explore what the experts have to say, what other men have shared, and what I have experienced, seen, and learned. I will provide you with the tools and a detailed map to help you navigate the incredible adventures of relationships and marriage.

I will point out common pitfalls and how you can avoid them, and I will prove to you that meaningful engagement in your relationship is the best time and energy investment for your health and income.

In this field guide, we will investigate difficult topics like money, sex, personal development, core beliefs, comparisons, love, patience, communication, and how to navigate these topics with honesty and openness.

I will help you discover the power of forgiveness and teach you to harness this superpower; you'll learn about the rewards of offering patience and understanding.

I can't lie; this journey *will* require change. Change that will make you stronger, wiser, and happier. This change can only be pursued for you—not her. You can't change her, but you can change yourself.

KNOWING WHAT LAYS AHEAD

Millions of men and couples are counting on their "special" connection to remain strong and special for all time, but they seek little to no relationship wisdom. Most men are operating off their own faulty and singular experience. They have neither been offered deep counsel nor have they attempted to explore the wealth of relationship knowledge available in books, articles, and the hearts and minds of other men.

This knowledge can be used as a roadmap to foresee upcoming obstacles and avoid them or plan for them. I have done my homework and studied the maps through and through: I don't want you leaving your relationship or marriage to chance. I want you to be prepared for the greatest journey of your life. Marriage can truly be a beautiful sanctuary with soft beaches for romance, adventure in the hilltops, and nourishment around every corner.

As I write this book, my wife and I are coming up on our twentieth anniversary. My curiosity and exploration of this topic began four years ago. It led to me reading, observing, conducting surveys, talking with numerous men, and undergoing a lot of my own self-discovery. Two years ago, at age forty-one, with eighteen years of marriage under my belt, I finally put pen to paper.

My marriage has always been pretty solid, and we grow stronger every day. But around us, we have watched as other marriages crumble. My heart has broken every time I walked alongside friends going through a divorce. Their experiences soon triggered fears that even my own children may one day experience this kind of devastation. This helpless feeling turned into curiosity which furthered my interest in exploring the complicated workings of a man's heart.

I started an organization called Modern Chivalry Men, pursued the best version of myself, and hoped to inspire other men along the way. I developed twelve core values for a man to live by and challenged myself and others to live them out. The values are Adventure, Courage, Courtesy, Empathy, Faith, Fearless Love, Honor, Justice, Leadership, Loyalty, Passion, and Truth. This pursuit resulted in positive life changes for me and many others as we engaged in our lives and the community. Through books, conversations, and personal discovery, I continue to search for what I feel has been missing for so many men, including myself, when it comes to marriage. So much of what is to come for you has been repeated time and time again, and little is shared about the journey. In this book, I am offering you a peek into the future. Marriage is not unlike any other epic adventure. It will be full of challenges and triumphs, but remember, you have what it takes, and I am in this with you.

I'm a suburban dad with three kids, three dogs, two guinea pigs, and four chickens (unless you are on my HOA board, then I don't know what you are talking about). I love God, my wife, my kids, my family, my friends, and the outdoors. We live in north Georgia, and both grew up in the Marietta area, a major suburb of Atlanta. We, however, love to always mention we lived in Fort Collins, Colorado, for four years, and it was one of the greatest adventures for our marriage and our family.

I've been in medical sales for twenty years. My bride has been in many different roles, but her passion is mainly for family and women's ministry. My kids are into cheer, basketball, and soccer. Nobody seems to love the outdoors as much as I do, but I drag them along whenever I can. I love to fish, and I don't care what I catch. I have spent many years going after bass but loved fly fishing in Colorado for trout. I just started exploring the rivers here in Georgia, and now I'm…hooked.

I did not grow up on faith and, in fact, was very anti-faith. But I would not be writing this if it were not for my pursuit of God, which began seven years ago. Alongside my marriage and being a father, finding my faith has been my most incredible adventure yet. This is, however, not a faith-based book, but I feel it's important you understand that is why I'm writing it. For years, I prayed for God to guide me and provide me wisdom—out of these prayers came my calling to explore my heart and men's hearts.

During my daily run, my mind would quickly slip into thinking about what it means to be a man, a husband, and a father. I would come home full of ideas and realizations that I felt the need to write down and share immediately. When I posted my musings online, members of Modern Chivalry Men (https://www.facebook.com/modernchivalrymen.org/) would message me saying "Thank You" or "I needed to hear that," or comments and shares that encouraged me that I was truly on to something. So, I hope you find that to be true for you as you read this book.

When I look at my marriage, I have been incredibly lucky, but not necessarily smart or strategic. I don't recall asking anyone what it takes to be a good man, let alone a good husband. I set out on this writing journey to capture the thoughts, ideas, experiences, and ultimately wisdom that my son, my future sons-in-law, and *you* will need to have a successful marriage. It's important to be armed with knowledge and understanding and not just luck. I want you to have more tools in your tool bag than I did and to learn from other men who have been through similar experiences. I want you to see the road ahead a bit more clearly and be prepared for a journey that will be unique but not so unique that other people's insight wouldn't be very helpful.

If you are like most men, you have learned about relationships only by observation—your father probably took a less than vocal approach on this topic, and that's presuming you had a father to observe in the first place. Most of us were given examples of how to be a husband and father by simply seeing what our fathers did or did not do. And now, suddenly, we are expected to be great fathers and husbands.

Imagine how this would play out at work. Could you be successful at your job today if you never asked questions or had any training? If you never had the opportunity to ask, "I don't get it, why did you do it that way?" or "Can you explain why?" you would certainly have a slim chance of being good at your job. I've been at the same job for two decades and still have questions. Marriage is no different; going into it with just observational knowledge will leave you lost, frustrated, and ready to quit.

This book is set up to be a thought-provoking guide to your early years before and after marriage. It is not a deep dive into the answers but a discussion to get you thinking. As men, let's be honest, we can be very prideful, and the world has told us we should have it all figured out and to "be the man."

There are three paths ahead after marriage: a loveless roommate situation, divorce, or a lifelong adventure with the woman of your dreams. This is your guide to make sure you stay on the right path. Let's get started; It's time for a little self-discovery.

CHAPTER 1:
Iron and Cotton

"When dealing with people, remember you are not dealing with creatures of logic, but with creatures of emotion." – Dale Carnegie

"Wisdom tends to grow in proportion to one's awareness of one's ignorance." – Anthony de Mello

"Experience is not what happens to you--it's how you interpret what happens to you." – Aldous Huxley

"Let's not forget that the little emotions are the great captains of our lives, and we obey them without realizing it." – Vincent van Gogh

MY FATHER AND MANY men his age carry a handkerchief and pocketknife. They carry after their fathers, who carried these tools everywhere. They keep them close to their bodies like we keep our phones and car keys near.

Over the years, I watched my father pull out his knife to cut any number of things. I have no doubt that his knife would be utilized along—with his big knuckles—to handle anyone who threatened him or his family. Any poor soul that made that bad decision would be left with a scar and a few less teeth. I'm lucky to have inherited those knuckles, so watch out.

The handkerchief was more often used to wipe sweat from his brow, soak up a woman's tear, catch a baby's spit up, or serve as a bandage. He later told me he carried two: one for him and one for others. The history of carrying two handkerchiefs dates back to the 1800s when kids carried one for "show and one for blow."[1] My father told me that he carried two handkerchiefs as a tribute to his father—who I never met. I am told we are very much alike.

In their footsteps, I carry a pocketknife and handkerchief to honor them. But I also carry them as talismans to remind me of what I should strive to offer everyone in my path: strength and compassion. The iron knife represents the sturdiness, strength, and protection needed from me. The cotton handkerchief represents the care, comfort, and compassion I must be ready to give. Together, they represent a principled life.

This concept gets to the core of what I believe is needed from every man. If we only offer up iron, we will only end up cutting. If we only offer up cotton, we won't provide the strength needed from us. The balance of iron and cotton is the key to providing everything we have to offer. To establish that balance, many of us, however, will require change.

For a knife to be formed, iron ore must be mined from the ground, it must be exposed to extreme heat, the impurities must be removed, and the carbon must be added. It is then hammered and shaped into the desired outcome.

You are no different. You have your origin, but are you ready to be hammered and shaped into something stronger? Something sharper? Are you ready to remove the impurities you once identified with and add in stronger, more beneficial elements? If so, understand now that this change will be hard, and in the end, you will be stronger for your wife, your family, yourself, and for all that cross your path.

If we can change and grow, so can our relationships. If we resist change, then we will watch as things change around us and maybe not for the better. Relationships should be resilient, not rigid. Many of the relationship troubles I have observed or been through myself happened due to resistance—men sticking to the firm narratives of their youth.

YOUR JUVENILE MENTOR

Would you go to a sixteen-year-old kid for financial advice? Would you go to a ten-year-old for spiritual advice? How about a thirteen-year-old for marriage counsel? Like it or not, we get advice from the young kid inside us every day, but we take it seriously because we think it's us: a grown, fully mature, adult man. As kids, we consciously or subconsciously formed opinions on diet, faith, money, love, world views, and marriage. These narratives and beliefs still drive our everyday decisions. Unless we step back and question them and what *version* of ourselves they are coming from, then we can expect to be lead astray. We likely challenge people's beliefs and opinions every day, but do you ever challenge yourself in a constructive way? We learned by observation, family, a sports coach, but rarely through a mentor and even more rarely by self-discovery.

A few years ago, I organized a handful of fundraising events, food drives, and charity dinners. One of those charity events involved a golf tournament supporting an addiction recovery program for men called No Longer Bound. This event led me to meet incredible men who know what it means to experience self-discovery and vulnerability. In my time with them, I heard many stories of neglect, abuse, false expectations, comparison, and unhealthy confidence.

They demonstrated to me the power of challenging the narratives we learn as a youth. They pursued understanding their faulty beliefs that stemmed from parents, friends, situations, and life events. Influences that were left unchallenged or even questioned. Instead of accepting their place in life, they started to pick only the stories that were useful to them. Now they could pick through their trials and tribulations and reprocess them in a way that put them to rest rather than repress them.

When most men go through something different or emotional, other men tell them to "toughen up," "get over it," or that "crying is for sissies." These phrases are designed to make sure you stuff down and crush any and all emotion. They are intended to harden you to the realities of life and prepare you for the battles ahead. For so long, our fathers have seen and told us that vulnerability and emotions are weaknesses. Generation after generation has done what they can to make sure men are strong, stable, confident, and not emotional.

It's no wonder we have trouble connecting with the women in our lives when they are wrestling with expressing emotions, while we wrestle with hiding them. We have not been trained or educated on how to handle those emotions for ourselves, let alone others.

EMOTIONAL INTELLIGENCE 2.0

In their book *Emotional Intelligence 2.0*, authors Travis Bradberry and Jean Greaves teach us that a strong Emotional Intelligence (EQ) is a better predictor of life success than the Intelligence Quotient (IQ). In their research, they found that out of 500,000 people, "only 36 percent can accurately identify their emotions. This means that roughly two-thirds of us are typically controlled by our emotions and are not skilled at spotting them and using them to our benefit."[2]

In my own survey of over sixty men, I found that over 80 percent of men received no direction from their fathers on how to interpret or handle their emotions. Most of us just watched our fathers, who said things like "toughen up." Add to that the comments about girls and women being dramatic, emotional, and the picture is painted for us. We hate weakness, and we will avoid looking weak—or feminine—so we face every situation with machismo instead of experiencing the full range of emotions that are within us all.

Dr. Gloria Willcox identified six core feelings[3] that we all contain: Anger, Disgust, Sadness, Happiness, Surprise, and Fear. These are the core emotions we all experience that can be further defined as she has done by creating her diagram, but let's stick to these high-level six emotions and discuss further.

Source: https://www.calm.com/blog/the-feelings-wheel

Most of us feel most vulnerable or weak when we are sad, fearful, or surprised (caught off guard). If we remove those emotions from our repertoire, then that leaves us with three go-to emotions: anger, disgust, and happiness. Two of those emotions—anger and disgust—may not be pretty, but they are assertive. Many men are running around armed ready to respond with two destructive emotions—anger and disgust—and only one positive emotion—happiness.

We typically handle fear, sadness, and surprise with anger or disgust. In short, at every turn, men are limiting themselves from having full-spectrum emotions. Add to that some bad history, and you have men who are on a hair-trigger to utilize anger over fear or disgust over sadness—over time, keeping our emotions down results in sarcasm, meanness, and aggression that can and does ruin relationships.

Like it or not, these six emotions are in us all, including that beautiful woman you are with. Burying those emotions under "strength" emotions could be the downfall of our relationships. Strength actually lies in the understanding of all six emotions and allowing them to exist. The understanding and mastering of our emotions can bring us the strength we truly desire. It's also the strength we will need to overcome the challenges life brings. It's the strength we need to offer everyone and, most importantly, to the woman we love.

I've learned more about compassion from women in my life, not men. A wealth of knowledge sits waiting for you as it did me from my mother, sister, my wife, my daughters, and upon discovering Brené Brown. Women's capacity for empathy and tenderness is unmatched and inspiring. So, who's your source for these essential tools? Can't think of a good source from your life? Then here are some tips for growing in this important area.

FIVE WAYS TO MAKE SURE YOU'RE CARRYING BOTH IRON AND COTTON

Emotions are the fuel that we pour into the gas tank of our marriage. Good fuel will keep things running, and bad fuel will only get us so far. So how far do you want to make it? I bet you want to make it to the end of this journey like I do. If so, then consider these five suggestions and explore this topic further.

1. Pick up the book *Emotional Intelligence 2.0* and take the test, which includes numerous questions to help pinpoint which of the sixty-six strategies will help you grow. It will reveal the behaviors you exhibit daily: Offer it to your wife or fiancé to take as well. If she won't, don't worry. You just take it and don't force it on her. It's time for *you* alone to learn about your emotions and grow stronger from them.

2. Study yourself: How often do you get angry? How often are you irritated? How often are you sarcastic? How often are you happy? Become a student of yourself and understand how you communicate.

3. Dig deeper into your emotions: I'm learning it's rarely the obvious stimulus that makes us emotional, and it's typically something deeper. For example, when I am failing at some sort of handyman task, it's not the dang tool slipping off the nut that is ticking me off; it's the fact that my pride is once again injured that a "real man" should be able to do this. Sometimes, though, it's just that my tools suck, and there is nothing deeper to it. Don't overthink *everything*. But maybe for you, it's jealousy at the root of why you are mad at her for being five minutes late rather than her tardiness. Or maybe you are irritated and sarcastic because you feel disappointed because you wanted to be having sex, but she was late. Has anger ever gotten any of us closer to sex? That chapter is coming soon.

4. Find some trusted advisors: This is the hardest one to accomplish because it takes some vulnerability. Find a man or men in your life you can count on that you can be real and authentic with. It's incredible to see men healed and empowered when they are honest and trusting with each other. Have the courage and the vulnerability to share what you are struggling with. If you don't have this resource, try to find one. If you can't, then tip #5 is for you. Getting support and being real is not weakness. It's a pathway to a better and stronger version of yourself.

5. Find a therapist. There is no shame in this. I've been to one, and it helped me overcome obstacles from my past, and I can't recommend it enough. You would go to a trainer to get stronger safely, right? You would go to a hitting coach if you were struggling with a fastball, right? Don't avoid getting help due to some perception of failure or weakness. We could *all* use some help, but it takes courage to admit it. Find a good therapist and let them help you discover the best version of yourself. Get forged in the fire of change and let the impurities fall aside. Add in elements that will make you stronger for you and for her.

Many of the next topics we will discuss are going to trigger emotions. Hard topics like money, sex, and your core beliefs have overwhelmed many marriages. In the course of your relationships, these loaded topics will ignite emotions, and conflict will often follow. Arguing and fighting can be healthy, but throwing bad emotional fuel on the fire can lead to both of you getting burned. I believe you have the strength—and emotional intelligence—to improve yourself, your communication, and your relationships.

It's time to get ready for change. Are you ready for the forging?

APPLYING IRON AND COTTON

- What significant event, experiences, or people shaped your beliefs on love, money, faith, worldviews, and health? How old were you? Make time to explore the beliefs formed in your youth.
- Are your emotions balanced like a finely tuned knife? What emotion/s need some further self-assessment and tuning?
- What was the last strong emotion you felt? Could you have handled it better, and if so, how?

CHAPTER 2:
Change is Coming

"Everyone thinks of changing the world, but no one thinks of changing himself." – Leo Tolstoy

"We but mirror the world. All the tendencies present in the outer world are to be found in the world of our body. If we could change ourselves, the tendencies in the world would also change. As a man changes his nature, so does the attitude of the world change towards him. This is the divine mystery supreme. A wonderful thing it is and the source of our happiness. We need not wait to see what others do." – Mahatma Gandhi

"Marriage changes us. Having children changes us. A career switch changes us. Age changes us. On top of everything else, marriage brings out and reveals traits in you that were there all along but were hidden from everyone including you, but now they are all seen by your spouse." – Timothy Keller in "The meaning of marriage"

AS A YOUNG KID, I was fascinated with underwater life. Every time my parents took me to the aquarium, I was glued to the glass like a Plecostomus (a suckerfish, for those without a home aquarium). Later, in my early twenties, I set a goal to visit every aquarium in the United States. My friend Zach joined me on my pursuit, and we made plans to knock out a few aquariums together.

In 2002, my wife and I were visiting California for Zach's brother's wedding, and we planned to visit the Monterey Bay Aquarium. Zach was tied up with family stuff, so my wife and I went without him. After Zach visited with some other members of the wedding party, we all talked about different exhibits we enjoyed. He eventually asked us if we were as impressed as he was with the penguin exhibit.

I laughed and said, "Nice try man, there was no penguin exhibit,"

He looked at me and said, "You didn't go to the floor with the penguin display? It was the best one we have ever seen."

Well, so much for my lifetime goal of seeing all the aquariums in the United States. I was peeved that I didn't do my homework ahead of time. I simply purchased the tickets and went without thinking about anything else. We winged it and just followed the flow of people and saw everything but the floor with the penguins. I went with limited knowledge and did not achieve my goal. I thought I had achieved my goal until I learned that I actually hadn't. I did not know there was another level to explore.

So, the question remains: how can we make it to the other levels of our marriages if we don't even know other levels exist? We might be settling for less, and we don't even know it.

How much of what you are experiencing in life is based on expectations and not based on your knowledge going in? How can we better prepare ourselves for the changes that marriage offers, the challenges, and joys? To start, we need to become better informed.

Understanding the phases of marriage and the strategies for success will prepare you better than most men. I'm going to help you plan your trip through the aquarium. Better to plan the trip now than be Googling "how to save my marriage" in a couple of years.

THE FOUR PHASES OF MARRIAGE

Let's start with a hard pill to swallow: many of your peers are going to go home to a failing or failed marriage.

According to a study by the University of Florida, 40 percent of couples eventually decide to get divorced.[4] If we don't want this to be us, we need to explore the ins and outs of marriage and our own psyches.

For those who resign themselves to unhappy marriages, the relationship becomes a roommate-type situation rather than a loving marriage. That is not what most people set out to do when they propose to their partner. How could we end up with a roommate instead of a loving spouse? Well, it happens to men who are not intentional and purposeful. You don't have to be one of those men: the tools you need are available, and I will lay them out for you. Learn about them and apply them daily in your relationships.

A lot of this book is about understanding milestones that most relationships go through. Below, you'll find the four phases that every marriage experiences in varying degrees and how to identify them.

PHASE 1: THE HONEYMOON PHASE

A time of attraction, passion, joy, and minimal conflict. The connection is strong and getting stronger.

PHASE 2: THE REALITY PHASE

Traits and habits are being revealed and are no longer hidden. Authentic natures are now exposed. Conflicts increase, and the connection is stress tested.

PHASE 3: THE ADJUSTMENT PHASE

Acceptance, rejection, growth, or compromises are being made based on traits, habits, and authentic selves. Connection and conflicts are fluid and changing.

PHASE 4: DECISION TIME

Based on the previous phases, the partners now make a decision about how to proceed.

A: Acceptance, peace, and rejuvenation of passion and joy. Connection is strong. Conflicts are well-managed.

B: Rejection, avoidance, and complacency. The partners are resigned to their sub-par relationship. There is minimal to no connection, or attempts to connect are abandoned. Conflicts are avoided or mismanaged. A continuation of Phase 3.

C: Conclusion of marriage. Divorce is the only solution.

Based on my research and my own observations, most couples continue Phase 3, the Adjustment Phase. Everything remains very fluid, and the same conflicts occur. Unfortunately, many of us have not seen or heard about couples in 4a. The research to get there has not been uncovered, or the role models have not been pursued. These couples are not perfect, but they are inspiring.

Phase 4b can be further described as the loveless and sexless marriage. A tragic outcome of neglect and fear in a relationship.

Phase 4c is likely familiar, but in many cases, it is a false conclusion if kids are involved. Depending on how amicable the divorce, it can be an expensive decision to stay in 4b.

The goal and what I want to provide a map to is 4a. I want my kids to find this phase, for you to discover it, and for my wife and I to stay there. This phase exists. The penguins have more than an awesome display for us to see. They are an example in nature of a lifetime of love in marriage. Penguins protect their mate, are monogamous, communicate well, and love to play. Understanding the stages of marriage and the strategies for success will prepare you better than most men. Men that are finding this knowledge later in life when they look up "how to save my marriage" or "marriage counseling" or "how to make your second marriage, not like your first." Let's discuss the early phases that shape up "decision time."

The Honeymoon Phase is incredible, but it's not so difficult to attain and remain in for a good length of time. Enjoy this phase as long as you can. Make memories and form bonds through adventures and intimacy. Pursue time together regularly, stay lighthearted on issues, and make connection your goal. Explore and discover each other. It's a great time to learn about childhoods, individual dreams, and goals as a couple. The next phase—reality—is inevitable, but it should be embraced, not feared. It's where real growth begins. It's where we train our relationship muscles to grow stronger.

The second phase is referred to as The Reality Phase because we are now juggling our relationship expectations, work, money, kids, and hobbies. Your vision for your marriage is playing out in real-time and in some areas conflicting with expectations. For her, it may be that your schedule still has not changed. You are still working long hours and getting time with buddies on the golf course. For you, it may be that she seems less interested in sex and is not tending to you and your home in the way your mother did.

Getting married did not change you or her, but somehow, it subconsciously changed expectations. Many of these expectations go unspoken. It's like taking a kid to an amusement park and having him wait in line for an hour only to be told he is too short to ride. Surely, that kind of information should be shared when you get in line, not when you get on the ride.

So, what information does she need? What do you need? Phase 2, the Reality Phase, is full of unspoken expectations. Full of unmet needs. It can be riddled with seeds of resentment waiting to grow into something bigger and more destructive.

I've been through this and walked with many men who have too. The Reality Phase is unavoidable and likely something you'll experience. Her desire for your attention and time and your desire for her support and intimacy are common obstacles during the reality phase. Meeting each other's needs is not done with enough intention and then gets missed regularly when work, kids, and hobbies become priorities.

I recall my early years of marriage as being the busiest I have ever been with work. I covered three states selling medical equipment. I was gone Tuesday through Friday consistently. Fortunately for us, our weekends were filled with quality time together. For some of my friends, the weekends were filled with more work or time spent with buddies and not their wives.

My friends and I had poker nights, golf, college football, fishing, camping, and money to finally put toward entertaining ourselves. I can't tell you how many late nights I spent with my friends playing Texas Hold'em. We were on the front end of the poker boom that took many men away from their wives. It was on TV, you could play online, and poker chip sets were selling like hotcakes. We all picked up a set and a table topper. We would organize small get-togethers with our wives and could not wait to ditch them to run to the basement to win back the twenty dollars we lost last week. It was all in good fun, and man, did we have fun. The drinking, the laughs, and the stories are still shared today. We were having a great time, but our priorities as young men with new jobs, toys, money, and wives were not always in the right order.

I wasn't at all concerned or thinking about what my wife's expectations were once we got married, and so began Phase 3, the Adjustment Phase. We goofed off as buddies like this before marriage; why should that change once we were married? Truly, what is the harm? The truth is, every outing I planned with buddies—golf, late-night poker, a beer at a bar, or getting a few hours of fishing in—was a decision not to be with her. I kept pursuing the fun I was having but not finding ways to include her. I was not making it a priority to get home at a decent time after the football game or a round of golf. She was not being chosen over these things any differently than before we were married. It was a light switch that did not go off for me until years later, when I felt the burning sting of her resentment.

Countless couples have ended the journey at Phase 3, the Adjustment Phase, thinking this must be as good as it gets. This must be all there is to see. They are wandering the halls of an aquarium with some pretty cool stuff, but they have no idea the best part even exists. They are growing bored or frustrated that they traveled all this way and the journey is not providing more. But instead of growing curious, they become resigned to it simply being an underwhelming aquarium.

In 2005, we were due for our second child. He decided that he was coming early, and we were in the hospital for a couple of days to have a C-Section birth. Our first baby was only a year and a half old at the time.

The first baby was rough. We had a preemie, and we struggled with her eating, sleeping, in addition to postpartum depression. A very unfair, unwanted, and very real chemical battle within my wife was raging, and I had no clue how to help her.

Our second child was a much smoother experience. We were home within a couple of days. Things were looking under control for the most part, at least from my male perspective. Her mom was there to help us, and we had done this before, so why would I cancel going golfing with my buddy for his birthday as scheduled? I didn't think it would be a big deal, and I couldn't let my best buddy down on his special day.

Well, fellas, that was a mistake. The mistake was choosing a buddy over my family and over my wife. My decision planted a tiny seed in her heart. That seed grew into a message that she was not at the top of my list, and neither was my new family.

Seeds seem so small and insignificant, but we know they can grow into something huge; all they need is time. As husbands, we have to be cautious about what seeds we plant early in our marriages. We must be careful and accountable for the seeds we planted in our relationship and that are now growing. We need to be conscious of the continual messages we send our wives when we choose work, friends, and hobbies over her and our family. And when those seeds turn into resentment, it's up to us to assess our own responsibility and not just think she is sensitive or dramatic.

Choosing to marry her will create change, but if you're serious about it, this change can be incredibly good for your life, your relationship with "the guys," for her, and for your family and community.

For the guys who think I am saying you need to give up golf, poker nights, college football season tickets, and so on, that is not the message. Your interests and hobbies are part of who you are. They help men release the pressures of work and family. The issues arise when it is a continual escape and not a joyful release. Women are intuitive, and they know if you are going out because you love your friends versus when you're going out to escape the house. It becomes a problem when it evolves into avoiding issues at home by spending time at the bar with a buddy or working long hours at work to avoid being present at home. Sadly, this story has played out for many, and they have left their wives and homes unattended.

What would your yard look like unattended? How would your car start to run and look if it was not maintained? Our wives, marriages, and family are far more precious than any yard or car. Yet, we will study the best fertilizer to use on the grass, but what about the best fertilizer for her to grow? We will ask about the best wax to get that new car shine. What about the best thing we can do to get our family to shine brightly?

In his critically acclaimed book *The Superior Man*, David Deida explains that men need to not look at their wife like a car that needs a carburetor maintained, but a flower that needs water. There is no great science here except to make sure your wife feels your love and has the space and attention to grow, not that you are just turning knobs and tightening screws in hopes she will suddenly be happy. She needs to feel you tending to her in order to grow.

Knowing these phases exist, what they contain, and what order they happen in will separate us from the men that are headed for failed marriages. We need to treat this like a hiker that sees the mountain peak ahead of him. The trail leading up to it is fun and easy, but then the incline gets steeper, and the air gets thinner. Despite the challenges along the way, the goal is to get to the top and see the view, and that should remain in focus through it all.

BE THE CHANGE

I believe we can change the divorce rate and marriage outcomes. With this book and other resources, we can all have marriages that thrive and not just survive. The tools are plentiful, and the study further describes how the successful are making it happen.

There are four general strategies that researchers Stephen F. Duncan, Geniel R. Childs, and Jeffry H. Larson found that led to more contentment in marriage:

1. Reading relationship books together.

2. Utilization of relationship websites.

3. Join or attend community or religious organizations that support marriages through events or messaging for couples.

4. Marriage counseling. (Many think this is what you do when you are in trouble in your marriage. I have learned that this is best utilized at any time during your marriage.)

The long quote leading into this chapter is by Mahatma Gandhi and addresses change in this world. You may have seen a shorter version of his quote, which goes, "Be the change you wish to see in this world." While he may not be the best role model for a happy marriage, his words offer a helpful truth that becomes clear when we change the word *world* to *marriage*. Below, I altered the full quote to drive this home:

We but mirror the marriages we have seen. All the tendencies present in the outer world of marriages are to be found in our lives and our marriages. If we could change our marriages, the tendencies in the world of marriages would also change. As a man changes his own nature, so does the attitude of the world change toward him. And his marriage. This is the divine mystery supreme. A wonderful thing it is and the source of our happiness in marriage. We need not wait to see what others do in their marriages.

You have what it takes to take on these changes. There is joy to be found in each change, but you will need to be intentional and purposeful throughout this epic journey.

APPLYING IRON AND COTTON

- What phase of your marriage are you in currently?

- What can you do to prepare for the coming changes?

- What expectations do you have that are unfair, unspoken, or unrealistic?

CHAPTER 3:
Intentional and Purposeful

"I did then what I knew how to do. Now that I know better, I do better". –
Maya Angelou

"An unintentional life accepts everything and does nothing. An intentional
life embraces only the things that will add to the mission of significance." –
John C Maxwell

"Wherever you are, be all there." – Jim Elliot

THE APPALACHIAN TRAIL (AT) is the longest hiking-only footpath
in the world, stretching over 2,000 miles from Georgia to Maine. It passes
through fourteen states and is a trail that only one in four finish. Hiking it from
start to finish takes at least six months to complete. Altogether, its elevation
changes are equivalent to hiking Mount Everest sixteen times! For anyone that
hikes, they know that finishing the AT is one of the greatest hiking accom-
plishments.

It is safe to assume that anyone who accomplished this journey without
losing any limbs probably did their homework. They undoubtedly asked a lot
of questions beforehand. And not just passively, they likely pursued conversations with other hikers relentlessly—especially people who had hiked it before.

They would need to research the gear needed and the food plans others used. They would need to understand the average miles per day hiked, the weather they would encounter, the shipping locations to send supplies along the way, and the types of dangers they could encounter. They would read books and would surely like and follow social media platforms on the AT and hiking. Above all, they would be in constant communication with their hiking partner to discuss, compromise, and agree on every aspect of this journey. While fear may creep in that they won't make it, that they won't finish the journey, they would not make plans to fail. In short, they would be intentional, purposeful, and prepared.

PLAN AHEAD

For many of us, our relationships and new marriages are very much like taking on the AT. We have dated and been in serious relationships, but none of them compare to the lifelong journey of marriage. We've had adventure, fun, hit some challenges, but it was all within our abilities. We can handle a short backpacking trip, but it would be unwise to think we are prepared to conquer the AT. Wildly, most of you reading this would probably spend more time planning for a back-packing trip than you did or will before getting married. The world's biggest and longest journey—marriage—gets minimal to no research by millions who decide to take it on. I was one of them.

How can we expect to succeed in our marriages if we don't do any reflec-tive thinking or research on the journey? How can we expect to enjoy or even survive if we don't know what to expect? Do you know the twists and turns where you're most likely to find danger? There are many people who can share with you what to watch out for and when but rarely do these discussions occur. These discussions could save your relationship from being torn apart like an angry black bear protecting its cubs. Research and the sharing of knowledge have probably saved many hikers from certain doom.

Years ago, I was a teen with a driver's license, a few buddies, some new outdoor gear, and a spring break on my calendar. We ended up hiking in the dark with no place to put down camp. A cold front pushed in, and it was the coldest night I have ever spent. With nothing thicker than a sweatshirt for each of us, we were done and called for rescue from our parents in the morning. We were confident we could handle the challenge, but it turns out this confidence was founded on very little experience and almost no wisdom gleaned from expert backpackers.

I went in thinking I knew all I needed to know. I had hiked before, but never this trail and never at this altitude. I was young and naïve. Nobody had poured into me any knowledge of the outdoors, and I did not seek it. My father was not an outdoorsman; that was my passion and hobby not his. I have learned many lessons through trial and error with my exploration of the outdoors. I have enough fishing blunders and outdoor examples of what not to do to fill an entire book. I rarely asked questions about the outdoors; I just went and did it.

A bear should have mauled me as many times as I kept food in my tent. I did not know you were supposed to hang your food in a bag up off the ground. I should have frozen and died in the woods not bringing the right gear or studying weather before a trip. I should still be stuck upside down in a kayak on a river teaching myself to Eskimo roll. Desire, luck, passion, and resilience are great for exploring the outdoors, but they likely won't help you navigate your marriage.

If you're anything like me: you love and adore this woman in your life. You want to see the two of you make it to the top of many mountains on your journey together. You want to overcome obstacles, create memories, and have a ton of fun along the way. That, fellas, is very much the journey I want to help you have. I want to arm you with information that you may not have sought—or that you may be too prideful to accept. I want you to walk confidently down the trail with awareness about what could come ahead and the different ways you can handle those obstacles.

LEARN FROM THE BEST LEAVE THE REST

Maybe you don't have a good example in your life to follow. I know men in your shoes, brother, and they are getting it done. They are becoming the men their fathers were not. They are becoming the husbands their wives desperately need and the men the world needs them to be. You have what it takes, but you may not have all the tools just yet. I know I didn't. Let this book arm you with some of the tools. Read it and absorb it. Make notes. Talk with others about it. Be uncommon with your pursuit of the best marriage. Be intentional and purposeful as if you are planning to take on the biggest journey of your life… because you are.

You will find most men are just making it up as they go. They are replicating actions and motions they learned from their fathers or worse from father figure examples on TV, movies, social media, or broken homes. Many of us have been polluted with ideas of what marriage should be. Our expectations have been set by false images, ideas, and comparisons. I'm here to remind you that you *can* be different, and no matter where you are on your journey, you can correct your course.

Strong marriages build strong families and communities. Your marriage is foundational to your happiness and health for you, your wife, and one day your children. A study published in the *National Library of Medicine*[5] looked at roughly 7,000 people and, over nine years, found the greatest predictor of life expectancy was not a diet, exercise, or medical care; it was the health of their relationships. Those who were in healthy relationships lived longer.

Have you ever heard those stories where a spouse dies shortly after they lose their partner? Think about that for a bit and let it marinate. Much like the AT, you need to prepare for this trek like your life depends on it.

APPLYING IRON AND COTTON

- Do you have the iron will to succeed in your relationship? If so, what does that mean to you?
- When was the last time you thoroughly prepared yourself? What can you take from that experience and apply to your marriage?
- What aspects of your marriage need purposeful focus? What are you possibly overlooking?

CHAPTER 4:
Love Her

"For love, we will climb mountains, cross seas, traverse desert sands, and endure untold hardships. Without love, mountains become unclimbable, seas uncrossable, deserts unbearable, and hardships our lot in life." – Gary Chapman

"The hard and deliberate work of knowing your spouse and loving him or her fittingly is foundational to any good marriage. Because our culture thinks of love as mainly an involuntary feeling and not a conscious action, this foundational skill is often missed entirely." – Timothy Keller in "The Meaning of Marriage"

You'll be my soft and sweet
I'll be your strong and steady
You'll be my glass of wine
I'll be your shot of whiskey
You'll be my sunny day
I'll be your shade tree
You'll be my honeysuckle
I'll be your honeybee
—Blake Shelton

DO YOU KNOW WHAT makes you feel loved? Can you describe the situations in which you feel most loved? And, to go even deeper, do you know *why* those situations make you feel loved? On the flip side, can you answer these questions on behalf of your partner? I hope you see why this is important.

I was in my late thirties before I started to get a far better understanding of love. A book arrived in my life called *The Five Love Languages: The Secret to Love That Lasts*. My wife loved to take those Facebook quizzes that ask you some questions and then decide whether you are a wolf or a flower, and other novel conclusions. Usually, I would just entertain her by filling out the forms, but this time, the test seemed more serious. It was about the variety of ways people give and receive love in relationships. I had never thought about it before and immediately picked up a copy of the book it was based on to understand more. The five love languages are:

- words of affirmation
- quality time
- receiving gifts
- acts of service
- physical touch

People can have more than one love language, but they usually have a primary.

For my wife, the quiz's conclusion could not have been more accurate: She feels loved most when provided words of affirmation and quality time. I, on the other hand, feel loved when provided physical touch and gifts. The final love language is acts of service, which was a lower score for her and low or non-existent for me. The keys to loving each other were right in front of us. The answers as clear as day on what she needs from me and what I need from her.

It is important to remember that you will instinctually want to communicate to your partner in *your* love language, which can lead to confusion in why they don't receive it so well. It's because you're literally speaking a different language. It wasn't long after taking this quiz that we realized we were giving each other what we wanted for ourselves. For example, I have been so fortunate to have a wife who offers me words of encouragement, but it's not at the top of what I need to be loved. It's what she needs. On the other side of the coin, I was going at loving her all wrong. I thought physical touch and providing gifts were going to kill it in the love department. For years, I would hug her, offer a massage, and pursue as much "play time" as possible. I would do my best to get her great gifts, and typically, at least according to her, I would get too much. It turns out I was missing her heart and in a big way. My desire for loving her well and making her happy was honorable, but it was like trying to shoot skeet with a pistol. I was using the wrong tool for the job.

The love languages concept and survey gave me the knowledge and tools to pursue her heart with more intentionality. I now purposefully call attention to the positive things my wife has accomplished in her day. I recently told her how impressed I was with how she handled a friend going through a hard time. I let her know that her heart for others inspires me. This genuine acknowledgment has fed her confidence and drawn us closer together. Her heart would no longer evade me now that I knew how to speak its language. Nothing would ever go wrong again.

Just kidding, her heart and I will absolutely have miscommunications again.

FIND CLARITY

Love languages are, to me, like shooting shotguns. For those of you who don't know the challenges of being right-handed and left-eye dominant, shooting skeet can be impossible. Looking across the barrel versus down has messed me up for years. I can only hit about every sixth clay tossed. That is probably about the same number of times I get loving my wife right. In the beginning of our relationship, it was more like nine out of ten because we were in the Honeymoon Phase; the romance and charitability was making us superhuman communicators. This phase, however, often camouflages true needs, which are revealed in the Reality Phase.

Over time, continually speaking the wrong love language is like being fed bread but no meat. It's nourishing, but you'll find yourself looking for more eventually. Unfortunately, love is not like food. It's not as obvious as realizing all you ate was carbs, and you feel tired, still hungry, and unfulfilled. You keep looking in the kitchen, wondering what you want. We don't want to stand at the refrigerator of our marriage wondering what will truly provide nourishment.

We need to know exactly what our partner needs to feel loved and fulfilled. We need to identify the go-to nourishment that renews and refreshes her. In turn, we need to be clear and honest with her about what we need to feel loved. Pursuing clarity and understanding will sustain you and her for a lifetime.

Clarity into how to love each other can move mountains in your relationship. It's where we establish a place of trust, a haven to go to and be renewed. It's the fuel that can keep each of you going and your marriage moving down the road.

Moods, pride, and distractions can get in the way of loving each other. Jobs, kids, and hobbies *will* take your eye off the ball, but the continual pursuit of clarity and understanding will ensure your partnership is resilient.

Continue to be a student of your wife. Her love languages may at the core stay the same, but how you need to acknowledge them and connect with her may change over time.

TEACH A MAN TO FISH

Have you ever had that experience where you're thinking about buying a certain car, and suddenly you see that car everywhere, at every stoplight? This shows that where our attention is focused can drastically change how we move through the world. Similarly, it's important to bear your heart to your partner, help her see your heart and its needs, so that out on the roads of life, she will have a new awareness of it, will see it everywhere, and understand it better. Give her that same gift. Ask her this simple question: What can I do to love you better? This question gives her the opportunity to set your attention straight and give your love a focus.

Focus is vital; otherwise, everything is blurry and glaring. As a fisherman, one of the essential pieces of gear you need is a pair of good, polarized sunglasses. Yes, it's important to protect your eyes, but polarized glasses help you see into the water with incredible clarity. They remove the confusing, frantic glare of the sun on the surface of the water. Sure, you could go out on the lake with no rod, no net, and no sunglasses, and trust that since you just *want* a fish, you'll catch one. But this is—for lack of a better word—crazy. Actually, that's the perfect word. A real fisherman is armed with more than just their desire; they lean into the knowledge, experience, and tools available to them.

Don't just go throwing a net, blinded by love; make sure you have removed distractions and attained focus so that you can find your wife's heart and reel it in with ease and control. Have you trained your eyes to see her? Have you donned the proverbial polarized sunglasses to see her heart as it is, without distraction? Do you know where to look among the scenery? Exploring and remembering tools like the Love Languages is equivalent to putting on a pair of polarized sunglasses. It can remove the glare from your eyes and hers.

The fact that you made it this far in the book means you are taking your relationship seriously. You're on track to become an expert in loving her. The Love Languages teach us that you can't be an expert on loving *in general*; you must become an expert on loving *her specifically*. This is the job for you to master and nobody else. Give her every tool she needs to love you fully and ask the same of her. She is yours, and you are hers, and nobody should love either of you better.

FEARLESS LOVE

Fear will absolutely limit your love for one another—fear of being exposed, vulnerable, and truly known. Stop equating vulnerability with weakness and start equating it with love. Fearless love will bless you with new levels of connection, understanding, and trust. If you overcome the fears that hold you back, it will lead you to a love that neither of you has seen or experienced.

It's time to be intentional and purposeful in your pursuit of this fearless love, don't expect it to just happen. The resources are plentiful, and your potential is limitless. Love is an action, not always a feeling. As Timothy Keller says in his book *The Meaning of Marriage*, "It is a mistake to think you must feel love to give it." This truth should be self-evident; you know your mom still loved you even when she did not like you. If you want to keep love alive in your relationship, you must love her even when she is unlovable.

Love is never tit-for-tat. True love does not come with conditions. I ask for your trust in this premise: Love fearlessly, and watch your love grow.

APPLYING IRON AND COTTON

- How do you currently express love for your wife? Is it what she needs, or is it a reflection of what you need?
- Can you be ironclad in your commitment to love her as she needs to be loved? If so, what will that look like moving forward?
- What is holding you back from loving fearlessly?

CHAPTER 5:
Passing and Dribbling

"We have two ears and one mouth so that we can listen twice as much as we speak." Epictetus

"Most people do not listen with the intent to understand; they listen with the intent to reply." – Stephen R. Covey

"You can practice shooting eight hours a day, but if your technique is wrong, then all you become is very good at shooting the wrong way. Get the fundamentals down, and the level of everything you do will rise." – Michael Jordan

---

I N BASKETBALL, PASSING AND dribbling are fundamental to the game. Mastering these skills and understanding their power is critical to playing well. In the sport of marriage, the fundamentals are listening and talking. Typically, when a couple asks what the key is to a solid relationship, they are provided with the response "good communication." But what is that? What does good communication actually entail?

Communication skills need to be continually worked on. If not, you risk forming bad habits, and this bad form will stay with you and your marriage.

Relationships are often described as being on each other's team, and teammates pass to one another seamlessly because they understand how another thinks, moves, and behaves. Good teammates make themselves available for a pass.

Great dribbling and passing is beautiful to watch. Conversely, it is absolutely painful to watch a team fail to dribble and pass well. This beauty or train wreck dynamic is also your options for listening and talking in your relationship.

I am sure you have seen it and experienced it. You know those days where it just seems like the two of you are on the same page? Your communication and understanding of each other just seem to be in lockstep. She knows where your head is, just like a midfielder knows where his striker is. You know what she is thinking, just like a point guard who sees the setup forming under the rim, and his star forward is making his move. Those times and moments in your relationship are when you two are at your best.

But what happens when the fundamentals start to break down? Suddenly, you find yourself talking when you should be listening – like a player that shot a pressured, deep three-pointer when he should have passed. You were daydreaming and not listening when you should have chimed in to support her – like a point guard dribbling and not seeing the pass under the basket for an easy layup.

HOW WE COMMUNICATE DEFINES US

I have a habit of interrupting my wife because I see the answer or know where she is going. I'm an impatient listener who jumps in before she finishes her story. Do you do this? I know plenty of buddies who do. It's one of those habits we need to kick to honor her and be there for her. So many times, she just needs us to listen. Don't worry; the answer will become clear whether you interject or not.

I know men who are very sarcastic and others who are very passive and silent. Whatever your communication style, make sure to stay aware of the ticks and habits that push her away rather than bring you two closer.

What does it take to form a communication habit? Research indicates it takes about two to three months to form a habit.[6] This means many of your habits are hard-wired based on years, not months. The good news is a new positive habit can be formed in a short time relatively. This is going to take some work and some assessment as we all have habits of communication.

What are your communication habits? Maybe there are good ones like making eye contact. Or maybe it's a bad one like mine of jumping off on a tangent as she tries to say something. Do you know if you are a good listener? Have you ever asked your wife? If you have never asked what it is like to be on the other side, now is definitely the time.

Are you more respectful in the way you communicate with colleagues than you are with the woman you love? Sometimes boundaries at work can be stronger than any boundary we set for ourselves at home, often because we never thought to set relationship boundaries for ourselves in the first place.

HOW WE ARGUE

A few years ago, I surveyed sixty men to gain insight into how their understanding of marriage and communication was shaped. One question uncovered that, when it came to marriage, approximately 80 percent of these men learned only by observation of their fathers and not by conversation.

This told me we should all assess what communication looked like at home growing up. How did your parents fight and communicate? What about your wife's parents? Was her dad verbally abusive to her mother, or was he a great listener or somewhere in between? What was your dad like? How much of that do you see in yourself? It's questions like these that will uncover so much about what drives your communication with each other.

When you were given the advice that "communication is key," did you simply dismiss it and say, "thanks, but we get each other" or "we have that part down?" You probably did. Well, you need to rethink this and ask yourself two challenging questions: Do you *actually* get each other? Do you *actually* have the communication part down?

For example, what did your last argument look like? Did you take time to understand her side of it, or was she just wrong and "being all emotional?" Does she better understand your perspective now? Has this argument come up again for the second, fifth, or even tenth time? On top of that, how well do you argue? Is it healthy arguing?

According to couple's therapist Wendi L. Dumbroff, there are three types of fighting. The first is when a couple has a dominant partner who makes the other shut down. The second is when both partners battle and create escalation. Finally, there are the couples that simply avoid conflict. Dumbroff worked with Dr. Holly Richmond and licensed therapist Jane Reardon to come up with seven recommendations[7] we should all consider if we want to fight productively:

1. Take a moment to pause
2. Beware of non-verbal communication (ex. Eye roll)
3. Stay in the present, don't bring up the past
4. Don't push harder than needed (Don't blow out of proportion)
5. Start from a "softer" place. (ex. Instead of an attack, share why you are hurt)
6. Apathy can be worse than fighting
7. Always seek to repair

An athlete who can dribble a ball in the open isn't as resilient and effective as an athlete who can dribble under pressure while being fouled. Similarly, most couples can communicate fine when everything is peachy, but when an argument puts you two under pressure, are you able to remember your fundamentals and keep your eye on the ball. There is no avoiding arguments, and—if executed well, it is healthy for couples to fight. An article in *Psychology Today* by Jennifer A. Samp, PhD, suggests that "facing the need to argue with a close other can be energizing and motivating—the topics that bring about arguments remind us of what is important to us, from our core values to our goals for a given day. Arguments also give us the opportunity to think about and voice how we feel about our relationships and 'who we are.'"[8]

During an argument, typically, one or both people feel they are not being understood. In many cases, unspoken expectations, fears, and worries have built up, and something small—even irrelevant—triggers it all to come up. This argument is demonstrating that this topic is important to one, if not both, of you. That somewhere along the way, communication broke down, and feelings got hurt. Take some deep breaths, a walk, or some sort of timeout if you feel really hot about an issue. If you can't, then try to count to ten in your head before you respond. Remember what you are fighting for: love. You want to love more after an argument. This is the crux of the aphorism: what doesn't kill you makes you stronger.

To build a stronger relationship, things have to get broken down. Like a muscle that is torn down and grows stronger when you work out, a well-handled argument can make your relationship stronger. A bad workout or argument, however, leads to injury and scars. Saying "I'm sorry" after an ugly fight where nobody really learned anything is not growth or healing. As Taylor Swift says, "Band-Aids don't fix bullet holes." (Sorry, I raised two girls.) That's the "cotton" side of my music taste.

THE STORIES WE TELL OURSELVES

I was probably forty years old when my wife and I discovered a great life hack provided by a well-known author, professor, and lecturer named Brené Brown. She shared a conversational tool[9] that has helped transform our communication with each other when it comes to tensions between us. It starts with the line, "The story I'm writing in my head is…"

In Brown's example, she talks about a great day at the lake with her husband. She was trying to engage with him as they swam around in the waters, but he was not engaging with her. The story she was forming in her head was that he was disappointed in how she looks in her bathing suit and some other small things that had happened earlier that day. The truth, however, was her husband was worried about all the boat traffic and their safety. When she confronted him with the story she was telling herself, it allowed him to quickly put her at ease by telling her the truth of the situation.

This outcome is far different than her just shutting down for the day and being passive-aggressive or getting angry and lashing out. It's a great life hack because it takes ownership of what is going on. It is not a blame game; it's a way of taking accountability and seeking the truth. It's an approach that leads with honesty and vulnerability so the two of you can understand each other better. This is where you can be a leader on the court of marriage. Try this multiple times and let her see you trying to connect with her. Let her see you trying to be accountable for your part of this game we play. Sometimes, you might trip or miss the shot, but as a teammate, she just needs to know you're trying to get better.

So, what stories have you written in your head lately? Are there stories that you assumed were true but never shared with her? Maybe they have to do with sex, or money, or jealousy? These are important and common topics. And like any stories we don't run by our partners, they can become toxic in our minds and infect our hearts.

The first key to interrupting these false stories is to simply be aware of them. Usually, these false stories result in negative feelings. So next time you have a negative feeling about a situation or something she does, ask yourself what your story is and present it to her not as fact but as a suggestion. Get her feedback on what is happening inside you, and you two can see if there are misconceptions at the root of your negative feeling rather than an *actual* issue. You'll find the story in your head was exactly that: just a story and not the truth.

COMMUNICATION TIPS AND TRICKS

The first step to better communication is to simply be aware of how and why you are communicating the way you are. Over time, if you practice, you and your wife can become much better communicators. Below are a couple of tips and tricks that I wish I knew from the start!

1. Don't offer a solution until asked, and only if asked
2. Actively listen, put distractions away
3. Be open-minded and try to picture and relate to what she is saying

4. Wait for a pause if you want to ask questions. Breathing is not a pause; refrain from jumping in until she is done with her thought.

5. If it's not a good time to talk, be honest with her and express that you can't give her your full attention but will at a later time.

SOUNDING BOARDS ARE BACKBOARDS

Unsolicited advice comes out as judgment. This is the number one mistake by the entire species of men and is well-documented. When your wife comes to you with a problem, always make sure to ask, "Do you need me to just listen right now, or are you looking for advice?" If she says, I need help: let'er rip. But in most cases, she'll probably answer, "Just listen." If that's the case, man o' man, get ready to shut down every solution that comes to your head. DON'T SAY IT! Trust me! I know you think you have the answer. All of us feel the same, but the truth is, she just needs you to listen. She'll ask if she needs help. Think of it as a chance to build trust with her, to build closeness with her.

If you can resist barging in with your answers, it will bring you closer. She will not walk away feeling stupid. That's right, by barging in with answers, you're not helping. You're making her think you don't think she can handle it or that she is being silly. Is that how you would want her thinking of you every time you have a problem? Relationships are about relating to someone else; in order to do that, you need to become attuned to your differences and how they interact with your own imperfect and peculiar psychology.

For many women, saying it out loud to you or others is part of her processing what she is experiencing. Once she hears herself say it, she'll probably come to the *right* answer all on her own. Remember—and this goes for most of life—there is rarely a *right* answer; there is only an imperfect answer that should *feel* right. Unless she is asking you specifically for an answer, she will come to a solution that *feels* right to her in good time.

You are often not and do not have the answer she is looking for. In these moments, your role is to be the backboard for her to get the ball back and make the shot on her own. So, be the backboard. If she decides to make you a player, then get in the game and give her your best. Until then, your role is the backboard, and that is all. Don't take the ball from her and make the shot.

Do you want to be the best team? Do you and your spouse want to make it to the finals? Then working on the fundamentals is key to your success. Identify your communication habits, root out false stories, listen, be vulnerable, and be intentional and purposeful about how you two communicate.

APPLYING IRON AND COTTON

- How would you rate your communication with your wife on a scale of 1-10 (1-bad, 10-Excellent)? What can you do to improve your side of the communication?
- What did your last argument look like? Has a common theme developed? What can you commit to do moving forward to create positive change and understanding?
- What stories have you created in your head recently? Are you treating her unfairly based on any of these unvalidated stories?

CHAPTER 6:
My Money Her Money

"I can live without money, but I cannot live without love." – Judy Garland

"Marriage is a partnership, and couples can't win with money unless they budget as a team." – Dave Ramsey

"No one person should feel like all the decision-making power sits with just the other party. It should be shared. For the long-term health of the relationship and for positive communication, you have to sit down and have a conversation." – Clark Howard

---

A FEW YEARS AGO, I was asked to talk to a young couple that was recently married. They were struggling to work through their differences when it came to money. I did not ask them about their portfolio, their debt, or their income. I asked them if they had ever discussed each other's financial past. I asked if they knew how the other grew up and what money looked like in their homes. They had not asked *any* of these questions. He did not know her money fears and anxieties were borne out of her personal experiences. She also had no clue what his family's relationship with money was.

Her experiences led her to shut down anytime the topic came up. In turn, he was quick to get angry, and a conversation that needed to happen never did. I asked her to share what from her past made this topic so hard. She shared courageously, and as my buddy listened, it was like melting ice with a torch. His anger melted away, and he softened his position immediately. His anger turned to compassion, and a conversation began.

Study after study shows that marital conflicts over money are more pervasive, last longer, and cause more damage than any other type of conflict. Money problems are often mishandled, leading to increased stress and depression.[10]

It maybe comes as no surprise that money is a stressful topic for couples, but how many of us have received solid, executable advice on how to be different? How many of us have researched the best ways to handle the topic of money? I bet several men reading this are thinking: "I already know how to manage our money," but that's the misunderstanding. It's important you know how to handle money, but when it comes to your relationship, it's more important that you know how to handle *conversations* about money. There are numerous resources for you to investigate setting budgets, goals, cutting spending, and investing. This chapter does not have enough room for all of that. This chapter is designed to help you navigate all those topics with far less frustration or anger. Your alignment on budgets and goals, for example, is going to take understanding. Saying "I'm right" and "your wrong" is a step down a long and difficult path.

IT'S ALL ABOUT THE QUESTIONS

In order to understand your wife's financial history, you've got to ask the right questions. What have been the milestones and bumps in her financial past? How did her family discuss money? What are her anxieties or excitements around money? Most importantly for you two, how does this history interact with your own relationship with money?

The answers to these questions could be the difference between retirement plans together or trying to figure out where to send the alimony check. I know this may sound simplistic, but what I have found is there is a lot of fighting but not a lot of understanding.

I'm guessing that as many of you are reading these questions, you can't help but interpret them as logistical questions: How much student loan debt does she have? How many credit cards does she have? But what I am really getting at is financial *experiences,* not details: family influences, fears, anxieties, desires, goals, habits, and wants. It's okay to have different financial plans, but in order to make a unified financial plan, you've both got to understand each other's relationship with money. Understanding debt is important, but what drives your spending and saving behaviors is even more critical.

Did she grow up with her parent's credit card in hand to use as needed? Did you? Did you grow up with a family that lived paycheck to paycheck? Did she? I have a buddy that has exactly this mismatch: His family was blue-collar, and they lived modestly and scraped for every penny. Very little was saved because it was all spent on bills, mortgage, sports, and higher education for their kids. His wife, on the other hand, grew up with little to no stress when it came to money. They took great trips, had nice cars, houses, and anything they wanted. Money was available and handled well. To no fault of their own, my buddy and his wife have different experiences with money. One is very concerned about a budget and saving for the future; the other sees the joys in living for the now and likes the niceties that life has to offer. Neither is right or wrong, just different and understandable based on their lives. The goal now is to make a financial plan that makes both people comfortable and excited about the future.

Instead of trying to decide who is right and who is wrong, you should instead seek to understand each other. Trying to figure out who was raised correctly on this topic will lead to arguments and continual frustration. Understanding will give a deeper appreciation for why each person does what they do and thinks the way they do about money. The best question to ask is what is right and wrong *for the two of you.* Examining the debt situation openly, what your current incomes provide and what mutual financial goals you have will provide you a far smoother path to your newly aligned goals.

It's important for both of you to recognize that you are not your parents and likely do not have the same jobs as your parents nor their exact income. You're also in a very different world, both economically and socially. So, you are not your parents. Your spending and saving habits are now dictated by the mutual alignment of you and your partner, not your parents and their history. Your parents provided you intel, and so did hers. Take what is helpful from this intel and leave the rest. It's the two of you against the world on this one.

FINANCIAL INFIDELITY

In his book *What do Radical Husbands Do*, Reggie Campbell coaches us to "burn the ships." It's a reference to Spanish conquistador Hernan Cortes arriving in the new world and telling his men to burn the ships on which they arrived. This was a clear message to his men that there is no going back. Campbell references this when he speaks about "other women."' He utilizes the idea to help men flush any idea of leaving their women for another if things are not going well. The same principle applies to finances. You both arrived with your individual boats called financial history, filled with cargo called debt, habit, preference, wants, needs, fears, and goals. These ships are full of your thoughts and ideas and not hers—she brought her own ship full of ideas and thoughts which are not yours. So, it's time to burn those ships and explore what this new land has to offer.

If we are resistant to communication, then we set ourselves up for financial infidelity. We'll cover actual infidelity in chapter twelve. Financial infidelity regularly occurs when couples are misaligned and miscommunicating. One study showed that "32 percent of their participants believe that some of their finances should remain private and off-limits to their spouse." Is that you? Is that her? Are you guys comfortable sharing *everything* about your finances? If not, then know that "76 percent of people said financial infidelity hurt their relationship and 10 percent said it led to divorce."[11]

Essentially, financial infidelity is hiding finances from your spouse. Whether you're lying about money you have or lying about how you spent money, you are committing a type of infidelity like any other. You need to stop acting like you still have a ship on the shore where you can store some belongings; you have burned that ship and are now starting a new life with your wife.

I committed some financial infidelity early on. I felt guilty for taking time away from my wife for fishing and the expense of rods, supplies, and so many cool lures. It was rare when I would have cash on me, but when I did, I would use it to pick up a few more lures "under the radar." The reality was this was silly. We never talked about it, and the story I created in my head was that she would be mad at me if she knew I bought more lures. She felt equally as bad getting beauty supplies. We were both hiding our spending because we had never talked about spending on ourselves. We just went off some "feel" of what was okay or too much. We did not create a ballpark dollar amount per month or any parameters. Somewhere along the way, we had established a big dollar threshold that anything over a designated amount should be discussed. Our discussion was very basic and left everything else open for interpretation—or misunderstanding.

So why would someone lie about money? Pride, shame, and fear are at the top of the list. Could selfishness be there too? What about boredom? These types of secretive spending are areas for discovery and discussion. Nobody wants to have to ask permission to spend money, but having transparency about how you tend to spend money is important for your financial future and, therefore, your relationship.

Maybe for the two of you, it truly needs to be a discussion on every dollar spent. You may be in a season of life or in a financial crunch where there needs to be some serious parameters set. It may be that you are doing okay, and you really need to loosen up a little and not judge her or create discussion on things she is buying. This journey is very specific for the two of you and nobody else. The only thing that ensures it's a smooth journey and doesn't ruin your relationship is that you are compassionate and honest, just like other parts of your relationship.

IT'S OKAY TO GET HELP

It may be a very difficult subject for you to discuss, or maybe you just don't know where to start. If so, then you might be ready to talk to a financial advisor. Talking to a professional helped my wife and me tremendously with our differences. I was very confident in our financial plan, but we weren't completely aligned. I'm more likely to spend, and she has a stronger desire to save. I would continually assure her that we were saving enough, but my words were not giving her what she needed. We had the same conversation again and again. Pulling in a third party helped us to get our goals aligned. It helped me to see that we did indeed need to save just a bit more to meet our future goals. It also helped her to be more comfortable with our spending. Getting outside counsel can be extremely helpful, but just make sure you get someone who is good at what they do and can help you two navigate the psychological aspects of these conversations. We had one bad financial planner, one okay one, and one great one. They are not all the same, and they have different ways they take a fee. Do your homework and ask others who they use and why.

MILLION DOLLAR MISTAKE

A real man should be able to provide for his family, right? Somewhere along the line, every man has developed this concept of provider; the one who makes it possible to afford a house, a car, cover the bills, and so on. This idea of provider has millions of men far more focused on work than they are on their family. I'm guilty of this, what about you? What if I told you that you are making a Million-Dollar Mistake?

The idea of provider is far more robust and complex than just making money to provide for your family. It's time to redefine "provider." The women in our lives need and want us to provide more than just money. In fact, ask her what she wants you to provide. I bet her answer includes the following: attention, stability, affection, adventure, and love. Yes, money is important, and you should pursue work and success, but not at *all* costs. You risk self-sabotaging your financial futures if all your focus is on providing financial security. That's the Million Dollar Mistake.

The concept of a Million Dollar Mistake was born out of a conversation with my friend and financial advisor Phil Adra at Four Corners Wealth Management. We were talking about the extreme costs of divorce.

In the below example, you will see what happens when someone invests heavily in work and minimally at home. This husband, let's call him John, then goes through a divorce. The second husband, let's call him Mark, invests at home *and* at work and remains married:

The below example and graph assumes the exact same background for John and Mark.

- forty-two years old with three kids and a $300,000 home
- Single income earner (helps keep the math simplified)
- $125,000 income and $150,000 in his 401(k) based on contributions since age twenty-two
- $50,000 Savings, $50,000 stocks
- Liabilities—$15,000 car loan, $200,000 mortgage
- 7 percent growth assumption on 401(k) and stock

Divorce Assumptions for John:

- Assets split 50/50 (i.e., $175K each)—401(k) cut in half, husband keeps house ($100K equity) in exchange for giving ex-wife 100% of cash and stocks ($100K total).
- Mandatory child support and alimony of $3,000/mo for eight years, $2,000/mo for two years, and $1,000/mo for two years for a total of $360,000.
- Lawyer fees are inconsistent for divorces but often substantial.

When John and Mark go to retire twenty-six years later, they will have drastically different retirement totals. John will have roughly $407,000 in 401(k). However, he will have spent $360,000 in child support and alimony conservatively. Mark, on the other hand, will have roughly $1,085,000 with his 401(k) and stock that he did not have to give up in a divorce. Plus, he paid no child support or alimony.

What appeared to be a $75,000 loss to 401K and $50,000 in stock at the time of the divorce is actually closer to a loss of $678,000 by the time he retires.

That difference plus the child support and alimony (–$360,000) provide us a million reasons to invest at home and not just work to be a provider. You need to make your marriage work.

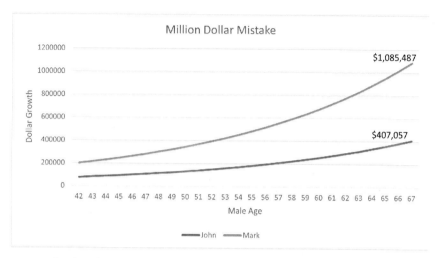

In this book, I mention a few times, and it's backed by studies that your relationships directly dictate your financial wellbeing and health. Don't make the Million Dollar Mistake of thinking being a typical "provider" is being the best husband you can be.

Every situation is unique, and I am not saying stay together because of money. I am simply pointing out that providing more than income can have a far better return on your investment. Just like the market, the earlier you invest and the more often you invest in your relationship, the higher the returns.

HAZARD SIGNS

If the news reported people getting attacked by bears on a specific trail, you would probably avoid that trail, right? If it could not be avoided, then you would at least go in prepared with bear spray or another line of defense. When it comes to finances and their relationship, I see men going down the same trail again and again to meet the same fate. And nobody is talking about it. Fathers, sons, and so on are either too prideful or just plain confused. The topic of money brings out something different in each of us, but we can be the men that handle it differently. We can be the ones who see the dangers and plan for them. We can find a different path to take and with her by our side.

In 2009, the National Council on Family Relations found that "Husbands and wives reported that they and their partners expressed more depressive behavior expressions (i.e., physical distress, withdrawal, sadness, and fear) during conflicts about money relative to other topics." The study specified that husbands, in particular, expressed anger during these conflicts more than their wives and more than any other topics. In general, the researchers found that these discussions were not generally associated with any positive emotions for men. It's important you understand your relationship with money so that these conversations can make you excited about the future with your wife rather than angry.

If we want to minimize defensiveness, sadness, and anger concerning money, we need to spend time on it. We need to communicate and foster an environment for our wives that is safe and welcoming. A lot of times, our issues with money are not *in the family* but rather in our relationship with the culture of money around us. Many people's Million-Dollar Mistakes aren't due to anything about their marriage but about external pressures to succeed and be wealthy. In the next chapter, we'll discuss how this distraction—this keeping up with the Joneses—can also be a costly mistake.

APPLYING IRON AND COTTON

- Where do you have your Iron firmly hammered into the ground when it comes to money? How is this impacting your relationship?
- What is the true source of your financial conflict? Do you know her history, fears, and goals with money?
- What questions can you ask and changes can you apply to better handle this topic? Where can you seek compromise?

CHAPTER 7:
The Thief of Joy

"We won't be distracted by comparison if we are captivated with purpose."
— Bob Goff

"Stay in your lane. Comparison kills creativity and joy." — Brené Brown

"Think about what you like about the Joneses, and let it inspire you to figure out how to raise your game in your financial life. Think of the changes you can make, the action you can take, the books you can read, and the guidance you can seek to get there," — Keren Eldad

"The reason we struggle with insecurity is because we compare our behind the scenes with everyone else's highlight reel."— Steve Furtick

HANDS RAISED HIGH WITH claws extended and mouth wide, fifteen feet of flickering terror stared at us from across the lawn. We looked upon this monster with awe and immediate envy. It was my neighbors' newest Halloween decoration, and my ten-year-old wanted us to get one too.

Caught up in the excitement, we immediately got on Amazon and searched "giant Halloween inflatables." With no regard to recent spending, we were deep into shopping. I didn't even for a moment think about the $1,900 quote for car repairs after my sixteen-year-old daughter backed into our minivan. Nope, not even a glance at the bank account to remind me we just gave our annual donation to our church. Within a matter of minutes, a $130 twelve-feet arched tree with pumpkins and ghouls was on its way to our house. Then it hit me:

keeping up with the Joneses was fresh and alive and all under the cover of fun and spooky terror.

I could go on and on with numerous examples of trips, toys, cars, houses, landscaping, clothes, furniture, decorations, and even socks. The world is full of things to envy—stuff to want and experiences to have. Our eyes are consuming, at a rapid pace, images of other people's lives and experiences on Facebook, Instagram, TV, and other platforms. Commercials, podcasts, and simple chats with friends lead us into believing that our next purchase or experience will fill us with the happiness we don't yet have. Surely doing what others are doing or buying what others have will fill our needs and make us happy. These things or experiences will help us now be seen as the men, the couple, or the family we crave to be.

Does spending money out of comparison really offer us the best relationship and life? Be forewarned, comparisons and envy quickly invade marriages.

THE ENVY GAME

Marriage brings a whole new dimension into the envy game. Growing up, it was all simple stuff like who had the better video game system. Now it's about cars, homes, jobs, and adventures—things that are far more expensive. A car or home investment can change your life for years. We often get sucked into what fellow couples are doing, and we want to do that too. We see pictures of a friend and his wife on a great vacation looking so happy; naturally, we want to do the same.

Our assessment of the friends we envy goes no deeper than seeing they are the same age and have similar likes. That's about all we need to know, right? What about their income levels? Do you make the same kind of money? What about their debt? Are they in debt? Are you? What about time off? Do you have the time off to spare? And even more importantly, is it even the trip the two of you would pick? Don't let others dictate your decisions through comparison. Pursue what makes the two of you happy.

Is it possible that "keeping up with Jones's is one reason that 78 percent of Americans are living paycheck to paycheck?"[12] I think so, what about you? The problem boils down to a lack of purpose and intention. Without goals and discipline, the comparison trap will become stickier than flypaper. It can be so easy to get caught up in the fun, but building up credit card debt and trying to figure out how you are going to pay the bills is not fun. Be assured, paycheck-to-paycheck living adds stress and pressure to your relationship.

The same poll also uncovered that 25 percent of people don't set aside any money for savings. Not saving money will multiply the stresses in your relationship when unexpected expenses like car repairs and a broken dishwasher occur. These are expenses that would otherwise be easily weathered with the cushion of savings. Without this cushion, your wife's fears and yours will start spilling out, and the arguments will erupt like a volcano. The fun you were having living carefree chasing the crowd can quickly lead you into surviving, not thriving. This makes it imperative that we invest our money and time where we can best grow ourselves and our relationships. Have fun but spend and save based on goals set and not out of comparison.

I recommend setting up financial parameters and questions. Here is an example to utilize: Before you spend, ask yourself three questions:

- Where did I get the idea to spend this money?
- Am I spending this money out of comparison?
- Would I choose to spend my money on this if there were nobody to compare to?

Financials are one area of comparison, and a big one that needs your attention. Like we discussed in the money chapter, we must stay focused on our goals. We need to learn to say "no" to comparison spending. Saying "no" is a powerful tool for every couple to utilize to stay out of this sticky trap. Saying "no" to comparison spending can be your weapon against debt, anxiety, and tensions in your relationship. Saying "no" will allow you to take control of your future together.

COMPARISONS IN OTHER REALMS

Comparisons aren't always about belongings and purchases; they can be about anything and are all dangerous. Keep watch for these and how they control you and dictate your relationship.

For example, will you compare her to her mom? Make sure you don't verbalize this. Many men continue to light that fuse by saying, "you're just like your mom." It's a mystery, but women don't like being compared to their moms. Even as wonderful as some moms are, that's a fuse we don't need to light.

The list will and does continue to grow. If you have kids, the comparisons come weekly, if not daily. When our kids were young, I recall the big comparison and competition of sight words. One mom shared her child had learned 120 sight words. Immediately, we were in a conversation and had a concern that our child only knew fifty sight words. The pace of children walking, talking, and potty training quickly becomes areas to compare. The one we are currently facing as I write this is how many AP classes does our high schooler have compared to others.

Our concerns about competition for colleges are becoming daily concerns and comparisons to juggle. The comparison trap is set for us every day. These comparisons immediately trigger fears and possible tensions. Unless a doctor or teacher is concerned about your child's development—and maybe even then— don't let comparisons take the joys of parenthood from you. Your kid will walk, talk, and stop pooping their pants when they are ready.

I came across a great article in *Better by Today* that flips the script on comparing. It said we should utilize our natural desire to compare and leverage it as a strength. The key is to find the right "mentors" to compare to.[13] To seek people that inspire you and not just compare to neighbors and friends. Maybe it's an older couple that you admire and have shaped a life that you wish to have one day. Find individuals or couples that you want to be like, not compete with.

We need to use this advice in all areas of our life and relationships, not just financials.

Unhealthy comparisons and competition can sabotage a relationship. Comparisons and jealousy regarding accolades, paychecks, and titles must be avoided with your wife as well. If we compare to her, feel inferior somehow, or are disappointed in ourselves, we are inviting discord. We will be creating a divide and out of our own selfish pride.

Plenty of women have higher titles and are out-earning their husbands. Our pride must be kept in check. Her success is your success, and your success is now her success. It would be like a star receiver being jealous of the quarterback for throwing a great pass to win the game. He is on your team; why would or should you be jealous? Your team is having success! Promotions, raises, and awards should be celebrated. If your wife gets a promotion and is now "higher ranked" than you based on title, income, or prestige, that is nothing to be jealous of. Celebrate it and crush that side of you that sees her as competition. Let it motivate you to up your game but treat it no different than watching a fellow teammate make a big play. Your teammate gave their best and made you part of a better team; now you get to do the same.

If this becomes your scenario, make sure you brag about her to your friends and family and make sure she knows how proud you are of her. She wants and needs you to be her biggest fan. Likewise, if you see her feeling resentful of your success, then have a conversation about it. Help her to see that you are a team.

What career she finds valuable and rewarding may not have chances for promotions and paychecks like yours. But it still needs to be treated as a vital part of the team. We need to absolutely keep this in mind for the women that stay home to raise our children. The measure of success comes in many forms—point out all her areas of success and be her biggest supporter.

Comparisons can truly be the thief of joy. Be watchful of these comparisons and the traps they will lay for the two of you. Traps come in many forms, and comparisons are simply one. The next chapter will cover other traps: negative influences that could take hold of you, her, and your relationship.

You, however, will be prepared. You will be different.

APPLYING IRON AND COTTON

- What did you purchase in the last year that was motivated by comparison?

- What unhealthy comparisons exist in your relationship? What comparison can you stop making?

- What comparison is currently motivating you, your wife, or your relationship?

CHAPTER 8:
Sex and Intimacy

Come take control, just grab a hold
Of my body and mind, soon we'll be making it, honey
I'll be feeling fine
You're my medicine, open up and let me in
Darling, you're so great, I can't wait for you to operate
…When I get this feeling
I need sexual healing
—Marvin Gay in his album Sexual Healing

"Your lips are like a scarlet thread, and your mouth is lovely…your neck is like the tower of David…your two breasts are like two fawns…I will go away to the mountain of myrrh and the hill of frankincense. You are altogether beautiful, my love; there is no flaw in you." – Songs of Solomon 4:3-7

"Sex is one of the greatest adventures in a relationship. It makes us feel alive. It can connect our bodies, brains, and hearts. In fact, sexual and emotional intimacy are intertwined; we need both to be happy. With too little eroticism-our relationship is dull and with too little emotional connection – sex is mechanical." – Laurie Watson, PhD, LMFT, Certified Sex Therapist

Podcast cohost of *FOREPLAY Radio – Couples and Sex Therapy*

"**T**HEY HAVE NUDE BEACHES," my teammate told me as we boarded a plane for Europe. I was fourteen years old and on a select soccer team about to play two tournaments in Denmark and Sweden. We would also travel to numerous other countries for sightseeing.

Little did I know I was going to learn about more than a foreign country; I was going to learn about the foreign land of the female body and sexual encounters. I was one of the youngest guys on the trip, surrounded by guys as old as nineteen. They knew far more than me about women, and they had hormones surging at a much higher rate. We were all excited about soccer, but the promise of nude beaches consumed us.

In Amsterdam, I followed along with the older guys. We dropped our bags at the hotel and headed directly to the beach. We didn't even change clothes. We took our shoes off, rolled up our jeans, and began our search for naked European women. We were disappointed immediately. The beach was empty. We picked up our pace and kept scanning. Our first encounter was less than desirable: We ran into some old people, then more old people, then more. Ugh, it was awful. Our dreams were shattered. Where are all the beautiful European women we had been told about? Then we spotted some.

Two girls were lying topless and the right side up. We did it. We found them.

But now what? The older guys engaged them in conversation. I was clearly just a young kid tagging along. These exotic half-naked women walked with us to town and stayed topless for the journey on the beach. It wasn't until we reached the edge of town that they covered up. We eventually had to go, but a dream had come to reality that day, and it was only the beginning.

We were exhausted from travel the first day, but the next night we had plenty of energy to explore Amsterdam. Trust me, all it takes is one night in Amsterdam to learn a lot about the female body and sex. I once again latched onto the older boys. I kept hearing them say something about the Red-Light District. I didn't know what that was, but that did not matter; I could tell by the way they were talking about it that it was a special place. These guys had proven to me they were brilliant and knew where to go to interact with women. So off we went into the night to see what we could find. It wasn't long before I saw the first signs of where we were going. A store I just passed had all kinds of pictures of naked women and signs that were shaped like boobs and penises.

The images started showing up everywhere. Then, I saw my first live sex worker standing in a window. She was dressed in lingerie, standing seductively next to a bowl of colorful condoms. There was a bed in the room behind her. The next window had another woman, then another, and it went on endlessly. Each street seemed to be an endless variety of women and rooms to "visit" with them.

It was unreal, and I was out of my depth. I had no idea what was going on, no words to describe what I was seeing. A few hours later, after seeing live peep shows, videos, and live sex workers everywhere, my education was on a fast track. One very odd, sexualized cartoon in some sort of sex museum still haunts my mind. That cartoon's actions and sexual encounters with every character changed cartoons for me forever. That was the beginning of my sex education and far more memorable than what they covered in school.

This epic journey was foundational to my sexual education and was a key trigger to pursue women more closely. I idolized the older boys and their experiences and gained what I thought was all the knowledge I needed to know. I left Europe feeling completely informed and confident I knew it all!

WHAT SEX ED LEFT OUT

What was your sex education like when you were growing up? Did you learn from a "wise" older brother? Did you just catch some movie scenes or watch porn? Did anyone share with you any insights on sex or intimacy? Were these insights harmful or helpful? That last question is probably the most important one.

For so many men, sex is talked about and treated more like a conquest than an intimate relation to someone else. A conversation with men that sounds no different than two guys talking about a video game: "What level did you get to?" "Are you done playing that game?" "Have you seen the new game? Can't wait to play it," and "I did this finishing move." We are often just kids with a new toy when it comes to women and sex.

Sure, we are all acquainted with sex by the time we are young men, but how much of our understanding involves the concept of intimacy? Intimacy is the most critical element to truly giving a woman satisfaction, and it's rarely, if ever, discussed. Most of us are armed with the knowledge of boys—not men. What I am offering in this chapter is the chance for you to become the men our women want, deserve, and need. A man that understands the key to sex is intimacy and does not have to demand sex or guilt his way there. This transition *will* require unraveling some of your myths, perceptions, and expectations.

It's not controversial to claim that the sex and intimacy depicted in movies, TV, social media, and porn are not the best examples for most people. The tricky part about this is what we see versus what she sees. There is a good chance she grew up watching princess movies, "chick flicks," and plenty of other fluffy romantic stuff. Her heart and head are filled with ideas of what you would and should do to pursue her affection.

Alternatively, men are typically influenced by friends, older siblings, commercials, seductive underwear catalogs, porn, daydreams, and powerful hormones triggered by a slight breeze. Surely, there will be no problems when you two approach the topic, right?

Maybe things are going well in this area, but do you think "well" just means "often"? What guideposts do you use to gauge your sex life? Are you going to rely on older brothers, videos, and movies? Maybe you should ask her what she needs in regards to intimacy. You should ask and understand what makes her feel wanted, needed, and ultimately satisfied? Her satisfaction, in the beginning, may have been having an orgasm, but time can change things.

Did you know that only 15 percent of women orgasm during penetration-only sex?[14] Most want and need more psychological and clitoral stimulation in order to climax. Many women don't know this either and think that there is something wrong with them. This lack of understanding and societal pressure leads to women "faking it." We don't want them faking it; we want them satisfied in whatever way that means to them. You have to ask.

In porn or movies, they show everyone at peak pleasure and make us feel like all love-making is fast and ravaging and perfect. It's implied that to be a "real" man, we should be able to get her to orgasm by a position we saw in a porn video or by pressing her against a wall like we saw in a movie.

Knowledge and understanding of what is truly desired is rarely discussed or passed on, so let me provide you a study to review.

A study published in the *National Library of Medicine* by Professor Debby Herbenick[15] outlined many findings that should be passed on to every man. Below are a few key stats to consider and possibly to help you unwind the myths offered to us by uninformed men, TV, movies, and porn. The first stat on this list should not be missed.

- 18.4 percent of women said vaginal penetration was sufficient.
- 62.8 percent wanted cuddling more often.
- 49.3 percent wanted more kissing during sex.
- 46.6 percent wanted to hear more sweet and romantic talk.
- 45.4 percent wanted gentle sex.
- 41.3 percent wanted the room to feel more romantic.

Keep in mind every woman is different, and that means it's up to you to discover how to love and satisfy her. I'll wrap this list up with one more stat. Almost 90 percent of the women in the above survey did not find watching porn appealing.

SEXUAL HEALING

In 1982, an incredible song for lovers hit the airwaves: Marvin Gaye's "Sexual Healing." Man, was it hot, and it still is! I would bet many couples are still setting the mood with this classic. Its notes and lyrics are seductive.

What I did not know was David Ritz, a well-known songwriter, told Gaye he needed some "sexual healing" after he and several of Gaye's friends discovered Gaye's large collection of pornography. Ritz then wrote the lyrics in an attempt to capture and allow Gaye to sing honestly about the addiction.[16]

There is no shame in admitting you have a porn addiction; the problem comes when you deny it or do nothing about it. The porn industry preys on men (and women) daily. They offer an escape and a fantasy that sucks men in by the millions. The imagery and the actions play out, and our minds are influenced by what we see and now desire. There is no mystery, and there is no pursuit, only satisfaction. As men, we take what we see and expect it in real life, only to find that the woman we love may have a different idea of what sex and intimacy look like.

"Studies have shown that porn stimulates the same areas of the brain as addictive drugs, making the brain release the same chemicals. And just like drugs, porn triggers pathways in the brain that cause craving, leading the users back for more and more extreme 'hits' to get high."[17]

For many, porn has laid out unfair expectations that your wife will never meet, or worse, that you are pressuring her into. These expectations will build up in our heads and leave everyone disappointed. These expectations can turn a loving relationship into one where she feels used, cheap, or like a failure. That is not intimacy, connection, and love: that is just sex and getting your rocks off.

I know many men who struggle with porn addiction—two of whom had their marriages forever damaged. One buddy of mine tells his story as a harmless tale of differing interests. They could rarely find a show they wanted to watch together and ended up in different rooms most evenings. For him, it was a show or some sort of online gaming. The time alone and distance from his wife led to an occasional look at porn, which turned into regular viewings. His wife discovered how much porn he was watching, and it resulted in enormous fighting and distrust. Another buddy got sucked into looking at porn regularly, and it pushed his wife over the edge to sleep with another man.

That is the short version of both stories. These marital tragedies slowly evolve over time when there is unknown history, undiscovered hurts, unmet needs, unspoken expectations, and a lack of purpose and intentions toward sex and intimacy. Like drugs and alcohol, porn is a vice we turn to when we are unhappy with something in our lives, and instead of putting in the work to uncover the issues and heal them, we just look for Band-Aids, which let the issues fester rather than heal.

LOVE LANGUAGES AND SEX

Intimacy, the most essential element of a healthy sex life, will never be learned online. It can only be found by learning more about each other, exploring her, and pursuing her. You will find pleasure beyond anything porn can offer if you focus on what feelings she desires rather than what feelings you desire. Imagine how strong and proud you would be if you knew exactly how to please your wife and fill her with sexual healing. I recommend returning to the chapter on love and really taking the time to figure out what her love language is. This will guide you to where intimacy can exist in your relationship and how you can improve.

Her love language may be words of affirmation: so, affirm her! Make sure she knows not just how sexy she is but how impressed you are with the overall woman she is. How talented she is not just in the bedroom but in life. Maybe her love language is quality time. So, offer her a break from tasks and create time for the two of you. Not just time in the bedroom, but time away from the distractions of work. Create time and space for her by postponing something on your calendar. She knows you want sex but honor her need for time with just you and let her decide what happens with no expectations. This will grow your connection, and her desire for you will follow. If you can get her to desire you more, then intimacy will grow, and sex will be inevitable.

THE HONEYMOON IS OVER

So, what can we do to ensure this connection is always present? How do we make sure that work, life changes, and kids don't interrupt sex and intimacy?

It's very common to find that after marriage, the frequency of sex drops off. The Honeymoon Phase has now faded, life gets busy, and distractions creep in. We come home from work ready to be with our wife, but she is not in the mood. She had a stressful day at work or is exhausted from taking care of the kids all day. We may see sex as the best way to unwind and disconnect from the stress, but for her, sex is way down on that list.

The expectations we set or that build up during The Honeymoon Phase are ultimately unfair. These expectations are not total fantasy, but they tend to be rigid rather than ready to change and adapt. We should absolutely want and crave intimacy with our wives. I assure you they want us to desire them and to continually see them as beautiful and sexy—but they are drawn closer to us when we understand their changes in mood, sexual drive, and priorities. She would love to be that carefree woman she was when you met, but that woman did not have this new demanding job or kids that are climbing all over her all day or both. So, we must evolve fellas. We must find ways to overcome these new challenges; we must seek intimacy with her now more than ever. But once again, you've got to burn the ship that brought you here.

CHANGES

Women are all different. Some have jobs and kids and remain very connected to you during many of life's changes. For others, things change, and intimacy gets challenged. Some women get unfairly affected by hormones and chemicals, leaving them struggling with depression. For others, self-image of their body after birth or with age affects their confidence. You may still see her as beautiful and desirable, but she may not feel that way. She may feel fat, ugly, and that's confirmed in her mind after comparing herself to other women. She may be convincing herself that you seeing her undressed would be a disappointment not just to you but to herself.

After childbirth, many women are all consumed by being a new mom. The sex that made this new little creature is far from her mind as she stresses about your child eating and sleeping. She is exhausted from late hours and simply from the stress of caring for a newborn.

There are many things women go through mentally and physically that we may never understand. These changes interrupt intimate connections, but that doesn't mean all intimacy must be lost. Still, it's important we are aware of how our sex lives can and will change.

For example, did you know that some men and even women suffer from a complex after birth called the Madonna-whore Complex? Essentially, it means the man or new mom sees herself as a mother now and no longer a sexual being.

Did you know breastfeeding produces a hormone called prolactin that can lower her desire and make her vagina dryer and thinner? That doesn't sound comfortable for her at all, does it? A variety of things could be impacting the two of you that need your patience and understanding.

Trust me, she does not want any of this or to disappoint you. She also doesn't want you to leave her during this time. She doesn't want you to seek satisfaction somewhere else or with someone else. She needs you now more than ever.

That woman that you have been with intimately is still there—that sexy, beautiful lioness has not gone, never to return. She simply needs a new kind of man to meet her where she is. A man who will make it through this change. A patient man, a strong man, and a man who helps her remember that she is still that incredibly beautiful, sexy, and desirable woman. What she does not need is a boy who demands or complains.

During times of change—and always, really—she needs compassion and understanding. These tools will help you find your way back together to lasting connection, intimacy, and sex. There are lulls, which is natural. However, with compassion and understanding, you will foster intimacy, and intimacy is key. It brings with it trust. It shows caring. It provides protection. It signals your everlasting commitment to her. You are in this for the long haul, and it's during times like this, you are building a stronger foundation for the two of you and your family.

Connecting intimately through sex is needed, healthy, and good for both of you. But what that looks like and how often it occurs will vary. For many of us to feel connected, we want and need time in the bedroom, and for her to get in the bedroom, she needs to feel connected to you first. This mismatch happens all the time. Focus more on connecting with where she is, and she will naturally be more interested in having sex because she is secure, chosen, and understood.

It may not sound sexy, but scheduling sex is another common recommendation when your lives get busy and distractions arise. Communicating this and your need for time with her may seem uncomfortable, but just imagine how uncomfortable discussing divorce could be.

Imagine how difficult and uncomfortable it will be to tell your children why mom and dad aren't together anymore. Talking about intimacy and sex calmly, curiously, and compassionately can be a key to finishing this journey well and providing a lifetime of connection, intimacy, and great sex.

APPLYING IRON AND COTTON

- What can you do differently to pursue intimacy and not just sex?
- What possible myths are you taking as the truth about sex?
- What's unhealthy or damaging your sex life? What aspect of this can you own and make a positive change?

CHAPTER 9:
Core Beliefs

"The next time your core beliefs are challenged - try being curious instead of furious." – Randy Gage

"Sometimes people hold a core belief that is very strong. When they are presented with evidence that works against that belief, the new evidence cannot be accepted. It would create a feeling that is extremely uncomfortable, called cognitive dissonance. And because it is so important to protect the core belief, they will rationalize, ignore and even deny anything that doesn't fit in with the core belief." – Frantz Fanon

CORE BELIEFS ARE BELIEFS we have formed through our own unique life experiences. They are beliefs that we continually seek to affirm truth in our life.

What if I told you the remaining chapters will be about *my* faith and how I want to wake you up to the actual truth? What if I was about to tell you that everything you were taught about faith was wrong? You would probably toss this book in the trash, right? I know I would.

That is because faith is an example of a core belief: a way of thinking about the world that is deeply rooted in your personality and understanding of life. These core beliefs are implanted in us through life experiences, environment, and possibly some research. These beliefs all relate to some sense of survival and stability of the world—challenging them feels like our survival and stability are being challenged because we hold them so deeply.

What I have found is that every person has five core beliefs that can lead to incredible connections or fierce battles in our relationships. These five core beliefs can be categorized as: Faith, Health, Money, Worldview, and Love. These beliefs are formed, solidified, and often don't change. Be prepared to be with someone who has their own set of beliefs that may not completely match up with yours; it's inevitable but not unmanageable.

BLOODY KNUCKLES

Do you remember Bloody Knuckles? That juvenile game where you exchange aggressive fist bumps until you or your buddy gives up because of fear, pain, or bloodshed. The idea was to see who was the toughest. Whoever dominated and withstood the pain won. This is how men often like to impose their core beliefs on other people. But this is probably not a game you would play with your wife.

Let's imagine each of these core beliefs as a finger on your hand. Your thumb is your Health, your index finger is your Faith, your middle finger is Money, your ring finger is your Worldview, and finally, your pinkie is Love. Now imagine offering your hand to your wife. Is it closed tight like a fist; do you want to smash her fist till it bleeds? Or do you want to open it up and be ready to be interlaced with hers? Which sort of relationship do you want?

Do you remember when you first started holding her hand, interlacing your fingers with hers as a sign of affection and connection? What were you offering her: a game of bloody knuckles or an offer of connection?

Art Courtesy of Prasad Weerasinghe, (weerasingheindi) fiverr artist, Sri Lanka

Our "hand in marriage" should be an offer, and accepting hers should be a promise. A promise to accept her as she is and what she will become. Our offer should be an open hand and not a closed fist. Our hand should be an offer to guide her and to be guided. This offering of our true selves will reveal our core beliefs and hers.

Offering is not taking or forcing. We are not entering into a lifelong commitment to take anything we want from her and demand she sees the world the same way we do. We are not offering to rule her with an iron fist; we are offering our hand to her to connect with her. Nothing feels better than walking hand in hand with the one you love; if you want a long and loving journey together, work on interlacing your core beliefs and defining a new normal.

THE NEW NORMAL

Our core beliefs are often how we define "normal," and anything outside of these beliefs seems abnormal. If your wife requests health food for lunch and we recommend burritos, and she gawks, we might be confused: "What, you don't think eating a bean burrito is healthy? My dad ate bean burritos every day of his life, and he is fine…it's perfectly normal."

We each come with what we believe to be normal: from spending money on your gym membership to how you love your kids. These will be potential sources of conflict because you are both offering your normal to the equation. Your current fights are probably exposing some of your conflicting "normals."

We have a choice to make every day. We can choose to battle for our normal and spiral down a path that can lead us to distance from each other and brokenness, or we can look to interlace our normals and find a new normal together. This new normal is defined by the two of you, not the rest of the world. Keep in mind this may require compromise by you and by her. Remain curious and explore this potential new normal with open eyes. This pursuit of a new normal will make the two of you more connected and stronger.

Let's take a deeper look into the core beliefs.

HEALTH

Health is broken down into diet and fitness. What you learned growing up and observing was surely different from what she learned. Did her parents workout regularly? Was every dinner followed with dessert? Were you a meat and potatoes kid, and she was a salad and soup girl when you met? Do either of you truly know what a balanced meal is? Do you believe working out is a priority, and she thinks it's fine just to get an occasional walk?

My wife and I had vastly different experiences with food growing up. For example, her mom and dad experimented in the kitchen. My mom kept it simple, and I don't think my dad prepared a single meal. My mother made sure we had meat (ham, fish sticks, chicken) and veggies (corn, peas, carrots, green beans). When my wife and I moved in with each other, my eating habits changed, and she introduced me to some great combinations of food I'd never experienced.

Health is a fantastic area to explore and a great way to connect with your wife. Whether it's cooking together, dieting together, working out together, or setting health goals—it's a meaningful way to define a new "normal" for the two of you and invest in a stronger, healthier future.

When we don't try to understand or explore each other's beliefs, we create and allow distance to grow.

FAITH

Faith is another area to explore—and it's a big one. What did faith look like at your home? How did it differ from hers? Is she Catholic, and you grew up agnostic? Or maybe you are an Atheist, and she is new age? There are numerous beliefs in the world, and these beliefs run deep. We all want to make sense of this life, so we find an answer that gives us comfort and control. We come into a relationship with deep-rooted thoughts on faith and religion. Faith was a very challenging topic for me and our relationship.

In our thirties, my wife's faith and mine created tension and conflict, and now it generates closeness. How did this happen? Like many core beliefs, having kids is what surfaced this topic for us. My wife and I both believed there was something greater than us, but it varied a bit on what we both believed. We did not attend church, nor did I want to. I had better things to do on Sunday. Like fishing! I would say this to people. "Would you rather me be in church thinking about fishing or fishing and thinking about God and nature?" The discussion continued for us, and finally, we set a New Years' resolution to go once a month to church. We wanted to simply expose the kids to the idea. Surprisingly, it sent us on a wild ride. My wife and daughter were quickly immersed, literally—they were baptized. Let's just say my faith was more like firewood. I wasn't seasoned enough to burn deeply for faith. I was too new and fresh and had not been exposed to the proper elements to make me a man of faith that burns brightly. I resisted and simply smoked; I was far from being ignited.

I think about fire and what it takes for it to burn and for a long time. It needs the right elements, the proper life breathed into it, and tending to keep it going. To throw me into the fire of faith too early would have been a mistake. I needed time—apparently seven years—to season this hardwood of a man. My journey led us to a few years of conflict. I was not comfortable or onboard with continual comments about God and Jesus in our home. It was fine on Sunday occasionally, but the topic of faith was coming up far more often than I wanted. I was firmly against numerous aspects of church and religion, but not totally. It's a very personal journey, and it would take far too many paragraphs to outline.

I will share, however, that my thoughts on faith were formed in my youth and by people that did not represent it well. Once that was identified and I became curious again, things began to change. This led to a new kind of closeness with my wife that I am forever thankful for.

Enough about me, what about you and what about her? What does your religious background entail? How different were your experiences, and were they good or bad?

Whatever occurred until now must be explored and together. Uncover each other's beliefs and determine as a household what faith will dictate in your relationship and your home together. Are you too firmly rooted to even consider her beliefs and perspectives? If so, that's a fist coming into your marriage, not the offering of your hand. This alignment will be particularly important once you have kids.

I used to say all the time, before I had kids, that I don't want to influence my kids with religion but to let them figure that out on their own. Where else do we do this, though? Do we let our kids figure out diet on their own? They would eat sweets all day. Do we let them figure out sleeping habits? They would be up all night. Do we let kids figure out dating and how to treat a girlfriend or boyfriend? We would have teen pregnancies left and right. I realized that guidance and curiosity to something so core as faith is better tended to than left alone. That fire may get out of control.

Go to her with an open mind and heart. Do you really have a right to tell her what is right or wrong with her beliefs? Would you accept her telling you what is right or wrong with yours?

MONEY

We won't spend much time on money since there is a whole chapter about it. But the reminder is to keep money from becoming a wedge and discover each other's backgrounds, habits, needs, wants, and get aligned on goals. Learn how to compromise and both get what you want financially: save and spend in a way that alleviates the tension around this subject. Be honest with your fears and try to understand hers.

WORLDVIEW

This could probably be summed up with the word politics, but I hate politics. Worldview extends beyond just the candidates and the media and what they are spewing from all sides. I am writing this during the 2020 election year, so my frustrations and disappointments in the media and politicians are at an all-time high. It's, however, very relevant and timely. This year has put much strain on relationships.

The marketing firm Wakefield Research conducted an in-depth survey of 1,000 people from around the United States and found that 11 percent of Americans, more than one out of every ten, have ended relationships over political clashes. They also found that twice as many (22 percent) millennials reported ending a romance over political disagreements. Many of these were over differing beliefs about President Donald Trump. Over 20 percent of people, and 35 percent of millennials, know a couple whose marriage or relationship has been negatively impacted, specifically due to President Trump's election.[18]

I'm not saying that you should give up your views, but don't allow a great relationship or marriage to end because you can't find a compromise on politics. This is not showing great strength; this is showing great fragility. You can be and are stronger than that. You can be the couple who seeks to understand each other, and that allows room for differences and unique perspectives.

Compromise and common ground are ideas and words rarely seen or heard by the media and politicians. Somehow, we have let the idea creep in that if you don't see it "my" way, then you are an awful person, hypocrite, or monster.

In a Hindu and Buddhist parable, six blind men argue about what the truth is about an elephant. They are all touching it in different parts: the trunk, the ear, the tusk, the tail, the leg, and the body. Each man proclaims that it is a giant cow, or snake, or a moving wall. But it was their combined truth—worldviews—that told the true story. Differing views can get hostile and create great divides, but your ability to remain curious, forgiving, and patient will get you through the simple and the most complicated times in marriage. These are skills that we will discuss in chapter eleven.

LOVE

As we used an entire chapter discussing how to love each other, I will use this space to point out a few areas where love can be a battleground or place to grow.

Some of us love our family, but we don't like them. Parents, stepparents, siblings, and extended family can often create tension in relationships. Your wife, for example, may have a volatile relationship with her father, but at her core, she loves her dad. Our desires to protect her result in her defending her dad against us. This is a core belief in family and love that needs to be honored and respected.

I'll test this with you. Have you ever spoken poorly about someone related to your wife and maybe even after she bashed them? How did that go? In my experience, the rules work as follows: You can talk bad about your own family, but if anyone else does, watch out! This fellas is where a core belief of love is being violated. You must respect her love for others but help her to build boundaries from toxic relationships. Maybe it's talking to her dad less often or only in the presence of you—keep your cool—or others. Support her in her struggles with family relationships. Be a safe place she can turn to and even let off steam with, but don't join in. Maybe even help her see that counseling is needed if this is a continual source of tension or pain for her and for your relationship

Parenting is another *normal* of love that needs your preparation. If you don't have kids, the prep you do now can save you from many battles in the future. This is where my wife and I battle most. We fight based on perceived *normals*, out of fear, and because of comparisons. Keep in mind that most everyone thinks the parenting they received was normal. So, we each bring our normal once again to the table. Simple things like Christmas traditions to complex topics like discipline are all potential arguments if not investigated and discussed. If you haven't asked yet, it's time for a fun discovery date night.

Below, you'll find some questions which can help you prepare for how the two of you will parent and where you need to pursue alignment. This topic, like marriage, needs far more prep and planning than the average man considers. There is not enough space in this book to give you all the tools you need. How you love and parent her children is of core importance to her as it should be for you. Seek information from family, mentors, books, and experts. How you were parented/loved was one source of input, and it's time to be open to other sources, including your new wife's.

Go in with an open mind and open hand. The fist is for fighting; it is not a tool of patience, understanding, and compromise. Make these questions fun, not an interrogation. This is a conversation, not a confrontation.

- What family traditions do you have?
- What traditions are you excited to keep or change?
- If we started a new tradition, what would it be?
- What did discipline look like growing up?
- What was the worst trouble you got in?
- How do you think we should discipline our kids?
- What would you like to keep the same or change about disciplining our kids?
- Who do you think we should go to for advice on parenting?
- Would you be open to reading parenting books together?
- Did you admire anyone's parents growing up? If so, who and why?
- What do you think our kids will blame us for?

Funny how we all blame our parents for something. My wife and I joke about this all the time. Too strict or not strict enough, kids will always think they know better. The key, and a hard lesson I have had to learn, is aligning with my wife; to have her back in front of the kids. As Abraham Lincoln said, "A house divided cannot stand."

Don't underestimate the power of these core beliefs and our personal ideas of *normal*. If they are not managed appropriately and discussed openly, they can and will be a continual source of strain.

My recently divorced friend told me about how he and his wife struggled over many issues. They fought often and to the point that they were separated several times. It was after their fourth separation that she shared with him that her parents had separated at least six times and that it was just normal for her. She explained that he should not be alarmed or upset because they will probably separate again. It was her understanding that going through multiple separations is just how marriages work. In this instance, clearly, her sense of *normal* needed to change a bit for them to maintain a healthy relationship. But this is the way that core beliefs can make or break a marriage.

Before we move to the next chapter, write down some questions to ask your wife. Try and be curious about her core beliefs, talk with her about them, and learn what motivates her in these areas.

Having these conversations as soon as possible will help you navigate the changes that are coming. These changes can bring you closer as a couple or push you two apart. Understanding each other's core beliefs will help you navigate these changes with your hands secured firmly and lovingly together.

APPLYING IRON AND COTTON

- Where is your fist closed? What core belief is creating a problem in your relationship?
- When and how were your core beliefs formed?
- What can you do to show more curiosity and facilitate a connection with your wife? How can you better honor her beliefs?

CHAPTER 10:
Under the Influence

"Without doubt, the most common weakness of all human beings is the habit of leaving their minds open to the negative influence of other people." – Napoleon Hill

"Keep the weeds of negative influence from your life. 'Farm' the seeds of constructive influence." – Jim Rohn

"Whoever walks with the wise becomes wise, but the companion of fools will suffer harm." – Proverbs 13:20

"Every single day in a marriage, we influence each other. It is a matter of am I going to have a positive influence or a negative influence?" – Gary Chapman

---

IN 1996, AFTER ELEVEN rounds, boxer Evander Holyfield beat Mike Tyson with a knockout. This enraged Tyson, and one year later, an epic rematch was scheduled. Little did Holyfield know his technical preparation wasn't going to be enough to avoid an injury that would last a lifetime.

The match date was set, and the fight was underway. Holyfield handled Tyson's attacks until the third round. Tyson, in all his rage, bit some of Holyfield's ear off. The fight continued, but Tyson bit him again. With Holyfield twice bitten, the match was called, and Tyson was disqualified. It was one of the most shocking events in sports history.

In marriage, as in boxing, there will be some threats you train for, foresee, and handle, and there will be other threats that leave you bloodied and blindsided. Some may scar you and your relationship forever. Watch for these attacks as they come in different forms.

Keep in mind real boxing (abuse) should never happen in your relationship. It's an analogy for you to remember to keep your guard up and to defend your wife and your relationship against attacks. If abuse has occurred or is occurring for either of you, seek counsel, and please review the disclaimer at the beginning of the book.

So, what attacks could be coming, and how do you prepare for something you can't foresee? Well, in the case of Tyson and Holyfield, it didn't come out of the blue. Tyson was resentful for a year. Where are you letting resentment grow? Where did an injury occur that was never addressed against you or against her?

I asked my wife if she could recall any of these attacks in our relationship. What did we allow into our marriage that festered and resulted in bloodshed? She reminded me about the resentment she felt when we had our first child—she resented that my life still had certain freedoms and hers suddenly did not. For the most part, my life had not significantly changed, but her world was completely changed. This admission was truly a sneak attack in the early years of our marriage, a punch to the gut of our marriage that lingered. I recalled many events as she reminded me of this time. I went to work, played golf with buddies, and hosted poker nights while she had a schedule dictated by our child's needs. I did not see it and was blind to the transition she was struggling with. It was a transition I surely would have struggled with as well if things were reversed. An exciting change to our lives brought with it an attack on our relationship. If we had both been prepared, we could have avoided or better managed the situation.

Where do you see these gut punches in your own relationship? Have they already happened? Do you feel like she resents you? Maybe it's time to ask and discuss before someone loses an ear unexpectedly.

Many attacks come in the unexpected form of influences. Subtle jabs at the foundation of your relationship, weakening the two of you. The following sections call out four key areas to train for, so nobody throws in the towel.

PARENTAL ADVISORY

I brought the idea of these "gut punches" up with a group of men I meet with. Three of them mentioned the influence of parents on their relationships—how they had been impacted by the continuous involvement of their parents and in-laws. As you might guess, these influences can be both profoundly positive and profoundly damaging. The stories they shared were often about overbearing mothers-in-law. Many shared about their wives still being heavily influenced by their fathers. While mostly well-intentioned, these influences can be invasive and destructive to your relationship.

When it comes to parents, a conversation about boundaries often needs to be had. These boundaries are set not out of disloyalty to your parents or hers but to protect the strongholds of your new marriage: a marriage that is yours, not theirs. In the words of journalist Mary Shmich, "Advice is a form of nostalgia. Dispensing it is a way of fishing the past from the disposal, wiping it off, painting over the ugly parts, and recycling it for more than it's worth." As such, much of the advice received from our parents on this topic is intended to help us be better than they were. The truth is, however, you are not them. Your relationship and your marriage are unique. Parents' wisdom should never be overlooked but assessed and applied where needed, not accepted blindly. Setting boundaries allows our relationships the room to develop their own rules rather than someone else's rules.

This is yet another conversation worth approaching with understanding and patience. Maybe she needs you to set a boundary for her from your mother—a mother-in-law that is continually questioning her and making her feel inadequate. Or maybe you need her to set a boundary with her father—the one she calls first about every decision in her life, even before she calls you. These are critical boundaries to discuss.

THE COMPANY YOU KEEP

Friend groups can be another big influence on your marriage.

We had a group of friends that wanted to go out all the time, and we found ourselves spending more money than we should. We had another group that was too raunchy for us. We had fun, but we realized every time we got together, there were tons of sexual jokes, and it was like a giant game of Cards Against Humanity. It was all super funny, but we always left feeling a little disappointed in ourselves. Then there are groups of friends that would rather spend time gossiping and feeling better about themselves at the expense of others. Our best friend groups have allowed us to simply be who we are. When we find that, it supports us as a couple, and we are confident those friends have our best interests at heart. It's nice to not worry about what they are saying after we leave. We have created great memories with our close friends. The company we keep as a couple will mold our behaviors and who we are becoming as a couple and as individuals.

There are a few questions I wish we had asked ourselves after spending some time with friends. Are we drinking more with this group? Are we spending more money? Are we growing closer together as a couple, or are we growing apart? Are we more cynical and sarcastic? Do we feel uplifted? Are we having fun life experiences? Are we worried they are talking poorly about us after we leave? Are we hesitant to leave each other alone with them?

We have one group of couples that have been with us since the beginning— three couples that would do anything for us and that we always feel comfortable with. The memories and the life experiences we have been through are remarkable. From marriages, births, divorces, and deaths, we have been there for each other. Fortunately for us, we also have another amazing couple that we met when we moved to Colorado. Lifelong friends that we now consider family. My hope for you is that you safeguard your marriage by surrounding it with couples that are invested in more than just the fun but all the joys and challenges ahead. These carefully chosen friends will uplift your marriage and help safeguard you from other attacks.

SOCIAL ADDICTION

More and more studies are coming out about the impacts of social media on our psyches and relationships. What was designed to connect us is actually harming thousands, if not millions, of marriages around the globe. One survey demonstrated that a "higher level of Facebook usage was associated with negative relationship outcomes." In addition, those relationships experienced "Facebook-related conflict."[19] Facebook usage has also been linked to increased feelings of jealousy[20] though it doesn't take a study to validate that one. We all know how addictive social media is—we are watching our partners spend time on their devices that they could be spending with us.

The science is plentiful around the dopamine hit we all get from it. That it's as addictive as a drug, and we justify the use and need as drug addicts do. It's a punch directly to the face of our marriage that we think we are strong enough to take. The rash of punches to our marriage daily and hourly is beating us all down, even if we deny it, continually. I've denied and probably will again and again. We have been through waves of this. There have been times where we have realized we are sitting in bed multiple nights in a row just scrolling through our feeds. Sitting so close, but miles away from each other.

One friend shared with me his realization that it was becoming a problem in his relationship. He confronted his wife the next time she was glued to the screen while they were sitting in bed together. She lashed out at him and was very defensive. She argued that it was her chance to "catch up" and to relax after a full day. He was defeated. He was trying to connect with her, and yet she was more interested in connecting with everyone but him. He is not alone, and this addiction is claiming more and more time from couples every day. Without barriers and plans to protect our marriages from this overwhelming desire, we will suffer a similar fate.

I've watched in my marriage how defensive we can be about this time spent. I've set limits of time on our phones only to simply approve myself more time when the timer goes off. Strategies to fight this plague on our marriage must continue. Our current society is trying to figure this one out. Studies, counseling, books, and conversations are coming out more and more, but it's like trying to quit smoking, alcohol, or even worse, someone telling me no more coffee. We cannot overlook or dismiss this one, brothers. It's an easy hole to slip into and get stuck in on our marriage journey. One of you may be in this hole or both of you. It will take your combined efforts to keep these attacks at bay.

There are tips out there for this one. Some include extremes of removing social media from your life. Others have recommendations of time spent. Another site suggests, down to the detail, things like removing ex-girlfriends. This is for you to explore together. How will you manage this attack on your relationship? If I could convince you for a moment that it is an attack, how would you suggest you defend against it? How would you utilize this tool to connect with others but safely? Maybe we treat it like a knife in the kitchen: It's dangerous but useful. Maybe like the kitchen knife never leaves the kitchen, our social media never enters the bedroom? My editor Josh Raab shared that he and his wife set each other's screen time passcodes. After the limit is reached, they have to request permission from each other. They often deny it and ask for quality time instead of more screen time. Whatever you do, consider that time on your devices might be harming your relationship and that perhaps you should take some action.

SMOOTH AS TENNESSEE WHISKEY

"Back down a country road, the girls are always hot, and the beer is ice cold…" I can hear this song by Jake Owen as summer closes in. I think there must be some unspoken rule of country music to sing about alcohol, women, summertime, or all of it at the same time. This song gets me excited about boating, barbecuing, and having a beer on a hot day. A cold beer compliments so many activities I enjoy, but does it compliment my relationship?

Do I really need to pull in all the stats that talk about how alcohol has ruined lives? You don't have to look far within your family, friends, or possibly a mirror to find an example. I'll focus on alcohol for a minute, but we can sub in drug abuse just the same. I think once again, we can't ignore what family history, genetics, and the influences of society are telling us here.

When I reflect on my history, I can't help but picture my legs in the air as a buddy counts loudly and a crowd cheers as I do a keg stand. That memory and my misplaced pride in getting people drunk for the first time in high school floods my mind. I recall hosting our senior party at my parent's vacant house and feeding people a vodka-infused watermelon that my buddy and I were so proud we created. We partied all night with Jolly Ranchers at the bottom of our Zimas. Senior year evolved to college stories, which paved my path for many work "meeting" stories during my twenty-year medical sales career.

My interest in alcohol was purely the pursuit of fun and out of the influence of my environment. I don't have a family history, and in fact, my parents never drank. The desire for me to drink simply matches my desire to have fun. A close friend of mine recently accused me of always trying to figure out how to have the most fun. Insert a beer, and, man, I bet I can get you to laugh, dance, and enhance whatever we are doing.

My caution to you—and a reminder to myself—comes from the last ten years of seeing past the fun and realizing the destruction I was witnessing as well. In my twenty-year career, I have watched as numerous marriages were destroyed by alcohol leading to infidelity. I've watched friends go to the bar instead of going home. I've heard men and women in recovery programs share their stories and close buddies share their own struggles. I watched one buddy in denial for years as he destroyed his marriage, job, and almost lost his kids because of alcohol abuse.

The stories and examples are endless, and you probably know a couple yourself. Society has moved away from concern here and often, if anything, celebrates alcohol. Take a moment and think about some of the memes you have seen, commercials, songs, and jokes that have us dismissively saying, "Well, I guess I'm an alcoholic, and it's okay." Alcohol consumption is not a joke; it is something to deeply assess.

The topic of alcohol and drugs is incredibly sensitive. It may even be the sixth core belief/normal you need to wrestle with. Are you defensive about this topic? Does it make you angry to think about anyone telling you to slow down your drinking? How would you respond if your wife said she is worried about how much you drink? Maybe it's a topic that you are sensitive to because you have seen the destruction. Will this be a source of tension because your new wife drinks a lot of wine? Maybe she was influenced by family or some equivalent show to "Cougar Town" with Courteney Cox, who made wine drinking for women look hilarious and desirable in many ways.

I've told my wife for years that I never want anyone to buy me alcohol as a gift. I thought about this a few times as I struggled to buy friends or colleagues a gift. I would think about what they like, and the first thing that would come to mind is how much they enjoyed drinking. I know we are far more interesting than that. Our relationships need protection from the influences of alcohol and drugs, influences that are incredibly powerful from our history, genetics, and society. Don't let alcohol consume your marriage as it has so many others. Decide who the master is. Are you the master, or are you being mastered?

The first step is to do a brutally honest assessment and not just once. This should be ongoing in your relationship. Simple questions like the following, to yourself and to your spouse, should be asked. There are numerous comprehensive resources to assist you and your wife with discovery and resolution to this societal issue.

- What did you grow up and see as normal? What did she see?
- Can I cut down on my consumption? Have I failed on this goal in the past?
- Is my work being impacted?
- How is my mood? Am I angry, withdrawn, or irritable?
- Are my wife and I drinking to cope? Is there another way we can handle it?
- Have I and do I continue to make unsafe decisions? Does she?
- How often do we fight when drinking?

- Do we continue to drink even though we know it's causing physical, interpersonal, or social problems?
- Does the thought of eliminating alcohol bring anger or anxiety?

Consider these questions and many more to root out a possible problem. Most things are fine in moderation, but is this hurting you or your relationship? Counseling may be needed and should not be feared. There is strength for you on the other side. I have seen redemption for men that battled this, and they are truly inspiring.

Dismissing and justifying are the go-to answers. Dig deeper than that and get aligned with your wife on this one. Decide how you will handle these topics and how you are going to watch out for each other.

From in-laws' intrusions to social media obsessions to substances, there are many influences that may impact you, her, and your relationship. These influences can be positive or negative, but if they are negative, they will win the fight with a knockout one day. Talk about these influences regularly and assess them diligently. Decide what boundaries need to be built and what needs to be excluded and included in your life. Figure out what enhances your relationship and what is hurting it. Determine what influences you are under. If we are driving our relationship under unhealthy influences, we are eventually going to wreck. A wreck that could leave us scarred or result in the death of something beautiful.

Utilize your strength and courage to protect what is most precious to you. Dodge, duck, and block the negative influences thrown your way. Know that you have what it takes to be a great defender of your wife and your relationship.

APPLYING IRON AND COTTON

- What is your honest assessment of the influences on you, your wife, and your relationship? What is your wife's perspective?

- What ideas can you agree on with your wife to protect your relationship from negative influences?

- What positive influences do you need or can you pursue to enhance your relationship?

CHAPTER 11:
The Big Three

"We are all so desperate to be understood, we forget to be understanding."
– Beau Taplin

"I don't know of anything more necessary in marriage than the ability to forgive fully, freely, unpunishingly, from the heart." – Timothy Keller in The Meaning of Marriage

"Our patience will achieve more than our force" – Edmund Burke

I N MAY 1943, DURING World War 2, a B-24 plane crashed into the ocean. Out of the eleven crew members, Lou Zamperini, an Olympic runner, was one of the three survivors. He and the other two survivors drifted for forty-seven days, covering roughly 2,000 miles. They withstood shark attacks, starvation, dehydration, and even an air attack by a Japanese fighter. On the thirty-third day, one of the men perished, and things were yet about to get worse.

The two men were picked up at sea by the Japanese Navy. This Olympic athlete who was poised to break the one-mile run record of a sub-four-minute mile was now a POW. Over the next two years, they would be starved, struggle with diseases, and beaten almost daily. Zamperini was a particular focus due to his fame as an Olympian. A notoriously wicked Japanese guard named Mutsuhiro Watanabe took much pleasure in torturing the former runner.

In the biography about Zamperini's life—*Unbroken* by Laura Hillenbrand—it is described how Zamperini was forced to hold a heavy beam above his head with the threat of execution if he dropped it. Further abuse came in the form of fellow inmates being made to punch him in the face until he was knocked unconscious. This continuous abuse was enough to break any man. Enough to make you angry at the world, God, and surely angry at your captors for the rest of your life. In the fall of 1945, the Japanese surrendered, and the POWs were sent home. For Zamperini, this was the beginning of daily and nightly torment that was battled with alcohol. A path of destruction for him and his marriage ensued. Along this path, he met Reverend Billy Graham and had his life turned around.

Five years after his release, he returned to Japan to face his captors, who were now in prison for their war crimes. He did the unthinkable, the unimaginable, and he forgave them. How could he forgive such violations against him and his fellow man? How could he even consider going back to face them if it were not to inflict justice and violence on the men that were so monstrous to him? Watanabe went into hiding and was never prosecuted. As Zamperini couldn't forgive him in person, he decided to write him a letter of forgiveness. Even though there was nowhere to send it, it was a letter that set Zamperini free at last, a letter that allowed him to move on and live his best life.

Similarly, inspiring stories abound. Jaycee Lee Dugard was kidnapped at age eleven and kept captive for eighteen years. She was abused continuously yet found a way to free herself by practicing forgiveness. In another powerful story, a mother forgave the boy who shot and killed her son. She went on to adopt him, and they have an incredible bond. Stories like these give me the courage and strength to forgive even when I don't feel like it.

Forgiveness is one of the Big Three tools you have in your bag to build a strong marriage. It's the sledgehammer of tools that can break down barriers that can form over time in our relationships. Most times, however, the sledgehammer is not even needed. The two other tools—patience and understanding—can be used instead to build a solid marriage.

PATIENCE

I bet Lou Zamperini discovered many emotional tools during his fateful crash and imprisonment. He was probably offered tools from other men and offered what he could in return. I bet anger was a tool used often. I bet hope was offered to him, and he shared it with others. I bet to our surprise; we would learn that humor was a tool pulled out to bear what must have been unbearable. As captives, Zamperini and his fellow inmates had to utilize many emotional tools to endure and overcome. One tool relevant to us, though, had to be patience. Imagine the difficulty of waiting at sea and then in prison to be rescued. A mastery of patience was learned but surely not wanted.

Patience is one of my biggest challenges in daily living, my marriage, with my kids, friends, and at work. I could not be more eager to get to the result, the solution, to the fun parts, or for my sandwich to get made. Recently, I was watching my sub sandwich be put together by a gloved employee. I felt my impatience boiling over as I watched her try to peel and place the meat on the bread. It's probably the most maddening thing to watch in this life experience. I mean, c'mon, stop counting the meat, grab it, and put it on there already.

But we need to be like a tape measure when it comes to our patience. Many men are not measured in their response to the issues that arise for themselves, their partners, and their relationship. It can be a similar type of anger or frustration every time, with little regard for the specifics of the situation or what memories their spouse may be reliving. Just like you would never use one measurement to hang things on your wall at home, there needs to be different measurements and patient responses for each scenario.

If you are like me, and patience does not come naturally, then it's going to take some intentionality to become more patient. You will need to first recognize when and where you become the most impatient. Is it when she tells a story? Is it a certain time of day? For many men, the transition from work to home is where patience is lost. It may be due to unmet expectations, tiredness, or a bad day at work that limits our patience. No matter the cause, it's a mindset change that must be addressed. In Regi Campbell's book *What Radical Husbands Do*, he suggests that when you come home, get within five feet of your wife for five minutes undistracted. To me, this is great advice to get calibrated with your wife. This purposeful interaction will help you gain alignment and clarity, set you up for providing patience, and immediately create a connection.

Imagine you come home tired or frustrated or both from work, and all you want is some peace and quiet in a clean house. Your wife had a similar day and wants the same, but on top of it, she had to handle an issue with your dog and got some news about her mom. Let's imagine two scenarios. One scenario is where you come home and pursue your peace and quiet only to be distracted and further agitated by an unpaid bill or a messy kitchen. In your lack of patience for these unmet expectations, you go into the "Why's" and "you's." You immediately pepper her with questions like "Why is this not done?" or "You should have taken care of this!" Comments and questions like these are a sign of your impatience, not her lack of care. In a second scenario, imagine you come home and spend the first five minutes learning about her day and seeing what kind of mood she is in. You bounce your eyes away from the messy kitchen and the bill that is still sitting out. You intentionally focus your attention on her. In those moments, you learn that after you left for work, the dog threw up, and she had to clean it up, making her late for work. Her boss then gave her a hard time all day. On her ride home, she got a text from her mom, who is anxious about a breast biopsy. When she got home, she sat on the phone, comforting her mom. What would be your reaction now? Would you have more patience and maybe help her clean the kitchen?

As you can guess by now, understanding your wife is incredibly important to the success of your marriage. Patience gives you and your mind space to be understanding. If you're impatient all the time, you're too busy focusing on the way things *should* or *could* be, and not enough time on understanding the way things *are*.

Alternatively, if you understand your spouse's personality, strengths, and weaknesses, you will naturally be more patient with her; in this way, these two tools are deeply intertwined.

UNDERSTANDING

The mystery of women and how they can react to certain scenarios has boggled many men's minds, including my own. Many other men and I have found ourselves muttering the phrases "She is just being irrational" or "her emotions are out of control."

With the birth of our first child, I stumbled into my own weakness when it came to being understanding. I recall the birth as being so sudden. She had an emergency C-section, and we were home with a preemie within seventy-two hours. Just like that, we were parents. We were tired, stressed, and she was recovering from major abdominal surgery. Something, however, was not right; my wife was not herself. It made me curious as to why she was acting so differently than I anticipated. Why was she not enjoying our new baby? Why was she so unhappy with this next step in our life? I was concerned and began to ask these questions and more.

We soon discovered my wife was wrestling with postpartum depression—an unfair chemical attack on her body was impacting her in a way I could not and did not understand. I determined it was now *our* battle to face, not just *hers alone*. It took me being compassionate, empathetic, curious, and most importantly—patient—to finally enter into a space of understanding.

This was understanding that I had not sought but truly fell into because of my love and concern for her. I am thankful to this day we took that on together and that I did not abandon her or get impatient and leave her to fight depression alone. I am confident we would not be together today if I had failed her during her desperate time of need.

Seeking to understand our spouses can be a flashlight in the dark that reveals what we need to know, but we must be willing to look. When tensions rise, and fights occur, we need to become curious rather than impatient. We can assume many things, but assuming is not going to lead us to understanding her better. Curiosity is the key that will open the door to understanding.

Over the years, I have observed that it is rarely the obvious stimulus that's causing us to fight. There is typically something deeper—past hurts, fears, and unforgiven wrongs. A simple miscommunication gets blown out of control. We aren't fighting because I did not take the trash out; we are fighting because I did not hear her ask me to take the trash out, and she grew up feeling unheard. Understanding these deeper reasons for why she gets upset will help you manage tension and fights but will require patience. Again, two tools deeply intertwined that will build the kind of marriage that stays alive with love and that can last a lifetime.

Growing your patience and understanding is foundational to the most powerful tool you have in your bag: Forgiveness

CHOOSING TO FORGIVE

At the beginning of the book, I promised that I would teach you about your superpower: forgiveness.

Earlier, I referred to forgiveness as the sledgehammer of emotional tools. Like Thor's hammer, forgiveness can break through any barrier you may be facing. If you wield it correctly, you can improve your relationship, life, and the lives of those around you. Let me demonstrate.

Everyone has wronged somebody, and many of us carry the weight of this guilt around with us. Imagine the person you wronged were to tell you, "You are forgiven." You cannot put measure to the power of these words. They are words that can lift unimaginable weights and breakthrough barriers you once thought were unmovable.

Forgiving someone who hurt you is a courageous act, not an act of weakness. It is a decision to pursue healing instead of perpetuating hate and revenge. Forgiveness can be difficult and may require support and counsel, but it may save more than just your relationship: it could save your life. Studies show that forgiving is linked to better health and a better quality of life. "Often people describe feeling lighter, like they have more bounce in their step, or that they again feel truly alive."[21]

Over the past few years, I have found there are times when even through my hurt or stubbornness, I have the power to forgive. If we wait until we "feel like it," it may never happen, and then we remain captive to the angst. "Carrying this hurt can be a burden to one's social, physical and mental wellbeing." (ibid) This is what modern psychologists mean when they repeat, "Move *through* your problems, not *around* them." Forgiveness allows us to face the complicated emotions that come up when love and hurt intertwine.

Forgiving does not mean that what happened was okay or that trust is magically reestablished, but it does establish a new starting point. That starting point may be where trust must be rebuilt, where boundaries are created, and where better communication is explored. Forgiveness offers the opportunity for something weak to be torn down and something strong built in its stead.

If we offer no grace, then we can expect only lies. If we create an environment where it's painful to tell the truth and forgiveness is withheld, then we are responsible for creating an environment where lies grow. If everyone is moving around their problems rather than stepping through them gracefully, the problems remain and fester.

Are you carrying anger with you over some past wrong—something you consider unforgivable? Harboring this anger will sabotage the man you need and want to be. Whether you like it or not, holding on to this anger ensures that the person who hurt you continues to hurt you every day; only through forgiving them will they release their hold on you.

In marriage, you will need to be able to forgive often. Simple frustrations and mistakes will happen every day, and forgiveness is the only way to ensure resentment doesn't build up.

Show love by forgiving those in your life.

STEADFAST MAN

Recently, a buddy shared with me his desperate need to escape from his wife and eldest daughter. Some heated conversations about current events had peaked, and he went running for the hills. The emotions, and dare I say drama, can be more than the average man can handle. Unfortunately, there is no escaping. We can get a reprieve at times, and that's where work, socializing, and hobbies can be utilized. Be careful, however, of using avoidance as your go-to option. Many divorced men today will tell you that long hours at work, time at the bar, and hobbies were major contributing factors to the downfall of their marriages. Fellas, we must get better at utilizing the tools we have: patience, understanding, and forgiveness. We need to be ready to stay, wade in, and not run away.

Tools are useless if we have no idea how to use them, though. For example, I still can't figure out how to use a voltmeter. My buddy just shakes his head at me every time I ask him to help me with an electrical issue on my boat. He has shown me a few times now, but I keep putting the voltmeter on the wrong setting and stabbing the wrong wire. It's embarrassing. Similarly, if we don't know how to pass and dribble, we won't be fun to play soccer or basketball with until we take those foundational skills seriously. You *are* patient, understanding, and forgiving; you just need some practice, so your teammate (spouse) knows you're in the game and not just going to run off the court when there is a foul.

With your continued pursuit of being intentional and purposeful, you will succeed where others have failed. The top of the mountain is in view, but we are not there yet. We must stay the course, and we must stay engaged!

APPLYING IRON AND COTTON

- When are you commonly impatient? What can you commit to do today to offer more patience in that area of your life?
- Where do you and your wife commonly misunderstand each other (needs, wants, money, sex)? What can you do to change this pattern?
- What are you still holding onto that needs the power of forgiveness to set you free? What do you need to apologize for and ask for forgiveness?

CHAPTER 12:
Stay Engaged

"Do what you did at the beginning of the relationship and there won't be an end." – Anthony Robbins

"Marriage is not 50-50. Divorce is 50-50. Marriage has to be 100-100. It isn't dividing everything in half, but giving everything you've got!"– Dave Willis

"Eliminate all your escape routes. Whether they exist in your mind, on Facebook, in your address book, or on the other side of town, you must seal off any open doors to other relationships. Your wife must become your only source of romance." – Regi Campbell in What Radical Husbands Do

IT WAS FINALLY MINE: a 1973 orange Volkswagen Beetle. My sister was off to college, and now it was my turn to take the wheel. I was sixteen years old and ready for adventure. Unfortunately, I needed to learn the stick shift first. My father was up for the challenge. We had a giant hill with a stop sign at the top that would give any newbie driver a panic attack. I remember the first time I had someone pull right up on my bumper at that stop sign. If you have never driven a stick before, then you have no idea how infuriating this is and motivating. I knew that if I did not manage the gear engagement correctly, I was going to roll back and mess up both our bumpers. I toe healed the brake and gas, revving the engine loudly. I released the clutch and launched out of that stop like a rocket. I shot out so quickly that my front two wheels came off the ground. I hadn't rolled back even a centimeter.

It was fun learning and experimenting with that car. My favorite thing to do was downshift into every stop. I don't recall replacing my brakes once in the time I owned that Volkswagen bug. I would drop down the gears like a professional race car driver coming into a turn; at least, that's how I felt. It would send out a deep growl and feel that I can still remember to this day. The car and I were one.

That feeling, however, was lost the day I moved on to an automatic transmission. Driving now feels routine and many times even bores me. Often, I will arrive somewhere and don't even recall the journey. I used to be engaged with every turn, and I was so connected to my car that it felt like an extension of my body. I realize now that I was far more engaged as a driver when my attention was on the details of the car. The stick, the clutch, the gears, and the gas all needed my attention. I was far more engaged with the journey and not just the destination when I drove that car.

Similarly, it's important not to let your marriage coast into automatic. Staying fully engaged—hands-on, manual—in the journey of your marriage is where you can be different than many men before you. Men who have allowed their relationships to be like a routine drive to work. Marriage is a vehicle that can bring you better health, adventure, protection, and even positively impact your income. Much like an old car, you tend to dutifully; your marriage will become more valuable the more time and love you put into it. If you forget about it and only do the sparse routine maintenance, it will just fall apart eventually. If you treat it well, keep it shiny and running smoothly, it will last you a lifetime and grow more valuable by the day.

Some men, however, stop doing the regular maintenance needed to keep this vehicle of marriage moving. Some treat their vehicles poorly, and others completely abandon the vehicle for another. Disengagement occurs often, and it is not always intentional.

When it comes to staying engaged, the three biggest obstacles marriages must overcome are work, kids, and temptation. Getting prepared for these in advance could be the key to finishing the journey together.

WORK

Career pursuits and increased responsibilities at work pull many men away from their relationships. I have seen many of these men in this pursuit work long hours and then quickly disappear to the golf course on the weekend. They do all this under the guise of providing for their families but providing, as we discussed in the money chapter, comes in many forms. Would your family and your relationship be stronger with a little less money as well as less stress? As time demands increase, many men subtract time from their wives and don't adjust the time spent with friends and hobbies. Rarely do we put our wives first. Women are forced to adjust and sacrifice to men's schedules, and their wants and needs are often dismissed. Quality time together goes unmanaged until it's time to re-engage or sex is pursued. It's typically in those moments that our neglect of the relationship becomes painfully evident.

If we continually find ways to disengage, how can we expect the vehicle of our marriage to move forward? It will constantly be stalling or out of gear. How can we expect it to be an enjoyable ride? We can't jump in the car whenever we want and get what we want out of it, with no maintenance or time invested.

Work is essential, and very few people will ever question that. Our value at work, however rewarding it may be and however important it makes us feel, does not compare to our importance to our wives and families. If you lost your job tomorrow, how long would it take them to replace you? Six weeks? Maybe three months? What did your company really lose, and how long until they recover? They may have lost some key clients, but they will get others. They may have lost "the big deal," but they will win another one. However, if you lose the job of husband, it's a ripple effect that does not impact some strangers for three months; it impacts the people closest to us and for a lifetime. Nobody can replace you, nor do you ever want them to. Earn income and titles at work, but remember, the most important title you will ever have is husband and maybe one day father. These are powerful titles to be proud of that last a lifetime.

Work is where many men run to feel validated and important. I'm guilty of this. At times, it's even easier to be a man at work than it is at home. Recognize this and realize that the work you do at home could reap far more rewards and joy than any title or paycheck. Staying engaged in both areas of your life is not always easy, but it's worth it.

As I have suggested in previous chapters, consider what you witnessed growing up. Did your parents continue to date each other? Did they dedicate time together, or did the world revolve around you and your siblings? Keep in mind, your parents sitting together at a sporting event cheering you on was important, but not the same as them finding time alone together, doing something they enjoy that brings them closer.

What did your wife see, and what expectations does she have? Did her dad neglect her mom, and she just thinks that's normal? It's time to decide what is the new normal and what you want for your relationship. It's time to be a man who has a plan to stay engaged with his wife.

KIDS

A young man we know came to my door the other day. He and his wife just had a child, and my wife and I peppered him with questions. We were excited for him and the next chapter of his life. He updated us on everyone's health and happiness. We know him well, and he's one of those rare open book kind of guys. He shared that he wasn't prepared for how time-consuming a baby could be and the attention that it would require from his wife. In short, he missed her. He cautiously admitted to being jealous and felt guilty about it. I shared with him how he is not alone in this feeling and that it happened to me and many other men. Many of us are not prepared for the transition either.

I recall that time in our life as being incredible, but I also recall an adjustment and some jealousy. It was a new gear we had to drop into, and I needed to learn how to find it. It was like trying to put my '73 Volkswagen into reverse. Now *that* was tricky; you had to push the stick down, left, and back. In the beginning, it was challenging to find that gear and stay in it, but I figured it out. Similarly, we can navigate these challenges and changes if we commit to staying engaged with her and our marriages.

Kids can bring many challenges and joys to you and your relationship. I recall when mine were little—you know, when the moms are still saying eighteen months instead of a year and a half or twenty-four months instead of two. That time is challenging because, for many men, we feel useless. If your wife is nursing or taken total ownership of so much of the baby's care, it can leave you feeling idle. Many of us may back off—but the trick is *not* to leave: just because we feel useless does not mean we are useless. The temptation to leave and entertain ourselves is strong, but this time is an opportunity to be present for her. This is a time when you can demonstrate your loyalty and love. If her love language is acts of service, you are about to score big. Being ready to suggest and provide her the rest she so desperately needs but is not willing to take. This is a great move. Assure her you can handle the children while she takes some time for herself. The simple question of "how can I help" will go a long way.

The next phase with kids is probably the most dangerous for the long-term vision of your relationship. It's a great phase and one to be excited about, but it's a phase that can become a time warp. When your kids go from age seven to seventeen, you will lose time. Time for you and your wife will be minimized and possibly disappear if you are not careful. Soccer practices, dance recitals, birthday parties, sleepovers, school plays, playdates, swim meets, and on and on it goes. My wife and I have three kids, and many times we tag in and out like WWE wrestlers coming and going from the ring (home). I wish I had tracked the hours and miles we have spent driving kids around to really articulate this point.

Let me pause to say this before you get the wrong impression: We love all of it. Well, maybe not those jumpy houses. In all seriousness, it brings us incredible joy to watch our kids grow and be a part of all these things. The message here is that if you are not careful, you will be like some men I know that are now looking up after ten to fifteen years of this and wondering who their wife is, and she is looking back wondering the same.

Pay attention to the tension of disconnection. As soon as you see it or feel it, you need to acknowledge it. Find a way to hit pause and reconnect with your wife and not just talk about the kids. Give her room to bring up issues about the kids and find ways to support her, but continue to dream together and make your relationship a priority.

If it's all about the kids, your relationship will wither. We have a running joke in our house since the kids always asked which kid we loved the most. I would make an announcement sharing that I love mommy the most. It was our playful reminder to them that we come first and that all of this would not exist without the love of mommy and daddy. We continue to share with them how important it is for us to continue to date and find time together and that one day we want the same for them and their partners. When they were little, they would sometimes cry when we went on dates and left them with the grandparents. We have found, though, that even a brief time away makes them appreciate us more. Your wife may struggle to leave them even for a few hours but help her to see the benefits for not just the two of you but for what you are modeling for them and their future. Research has shown that the best thing we can do for our children is to provide them a stable home, not just income and things.

I wish I could set an alarm on this book to go off every month for those ten to fifteen years for you. If months turn into years and you are not continuing to date your wife, there will be no future for you two when the kids are gone. This is a common pitfall that will undoubtedly lead you into the phrase we so often hear... "we just grew apart."

Our kids have brought us so much joy, and together, we love watching them grow up, so much so that we are often consumed by their daily activities, sports, and overall needs. Like many couples, we get lost in the time warp and sometimes for a few weeks before one of us realizes our need to connect. Stay attentive and engaged.

The addition of a child, extra time at work, and other life changes can lead to both of your needs not being met. When needs go unmet, someone usually becomes vulnerable.

TEMPTATION

Lack of engagement leads to being easily tempted by shiny objects, which opens the doors to infidelity. To ensure this does not happen, we need to do our part, once again, to "burn the ships." We need to remove any escape plans and consideration of being with another woman or some other fantasy life. *This* is the path we are on, *this* is our family, *this* is our job, stop looking to the horizon every time the going gets tough; Atlantis is not out there.

Infidelity in our marriage is obviously not what we want. According to a national survey by the American Association for Marriage and Family Therapy, 15 percent of married women and 25 percent of married men have had extramarital affairs.[22]

An article in *Psychology Today* identified the top reasons for infidelity: falling out of love, seeking variety, and feeling neglected. Other reasons included situational forces, desire to raise self-esteem, and anger with a partner.[23]

I arm you with this knowledge so you can be prepared, not fearful or jealous. Knowing what causes men and women to be unfaithful is information we can use to safeguard our relationships. Building these critical safeguards in our relationship cannot be done without open and honest communication. This is where we need to get uncomfortable and be vulnerable and ready to share.

We need to have the courage to talk to our partner not just once but throughout our relationship. We need to tell them to come to us if they feel neglected, unloved, or if they need variety. We need to offer a safe place for this conversation to occur that is free of judgment, jealousy, and anger.

We need them to know that we want to help them get their needs met. We need to invite that conversation. We also need to be truthful about what needs are not being met for us before that leads to seeking them elsewhere. Maybe you think that's too uncomfortable of a conversation to have?

What is more uncomfortable—getting caught cheating or being honest about your temptations? This is why it is critical to build a marriage where open communication is invited and received with patience and understanding.

I have men and women in my life who have been down the road of infidelity. It's beyond uncomfortable; it will absolutely rip your guts out. Affairs offer the fantasy that fulfillment will be found somewhere else, when in fact, affairs lead to brokenness and pain. As reported in *Psychology Today*, affairs are a form of escape that is seeking renewal, rejuvenation, and joy but leads to depression, anxiety, and domestic violence.

Being with another woman is like jumping off a cliff and not having a parachute. It may be exhilarating for a little while, but that ride is going to end terribly and not just for the one who jumped.

Dave Willis, the author of *Secrets to a Stronger Marriage*, provides us with this sound advice: "Be VERY careful about having friends of the opposite sex. If you have a 'friend' that you tell things to that you don't tell your spouse, then you are creating a toxic situation. Affairs don't start in the bedroom; they start with conversations, emails, texts, and communication that lead down a dangerous path. Protect your Marriage!"

KEEP DATING HER

My wife and I unintentionally did a good job of dating each other after marriage. However, we hit some slumps, and our dating became routine. I loved the movies, and she loved trying new foods. The standard dinner and a movie were our go-to, but after years of her falling asleep in movies and going back to the same places to eat, we grew bored. Our dates were frequently canceled, and we opted to stay in instead. Fortunately, we knew we needed to change things up. We introduced a few new elements into our dating, and it truly spiced up our time together.

One addition to our date nights was seeking out bands playing at small venues. It has energized our alone time together and has grown our connection. The great thing about concerts is not just the date night itself, but all that leads up to it and everything after. Searching for the bands, getting the tickets, and the anticipation all make for great fun. After the concert and for years, we now reminisce about the fun we had. When we hear one of the songs of the bands we went to see, we are both instantly connected to that fun night together. Seeking concerts was one big and favorite change we made, but not the only one. We started to make it a point to find time away together throughout the year. Just a few nights away from the kids provides us the nourishment and refreshment we so badly crave from one another. It's been as simple as a hotel downtown or more involved like a flight to Colorado to go ski together. The time away and investment in each other is worth every penny.

With the addition of kids, these nights away have been incredibly import-ant. So often, the new titles of Mom and Dad replace who we are as Mr. and Mrs. Many of our wives are now regularly called mommy, and that is not a title that reminds her of her independence, beauty, and sexiness. Time away provides those reminders and allows the two of you to build connection.

There are many ways to stay engaged during the week. Outlined below are some suggestions, but the list is endless. Sit down with her and make a list together and be open to trying something new:

Cooking	Dieting	Exercising	Hiking
Evening walk	Reading together	Shopping	Bathing together
Time to talk	Boating	Fishing	Dancing
Concerts	Dinner out	Double date	Theatre

Being intentional, purposeful, and engaged during career advancements, a baby, and any life change will fortify your marriage. It will set you up for the happi-ness, connection, and intimacy you both desire. Staying engaged will ensure that your love grows, not dies, and it will set you up to be the couple that finishes the journey together and happily. You can be the one in four that finishes the AT of Marriage, so stay engaged with her and enjoy the journey ahead.

APPLYING IRON AND COTTON

- Where have you already disengaged? How can you re-engage?

- What new date idea or time together can you commit to this week? This month? This year?

- Where have you let temptation creep in? What can you do today to eliminate that temptation? What new boundary can you create for yourself?

CONCLUSION

"When a man truly commits, the universe will conspire to assure his success."
– Henry David Thoreau.

"Life is a journey, and if you fall in love with the journey, you will be in love forever" – Peter Hagerty

"Relationships don't last because of the good times; they last because the hard times were handled with love and care." – Anmol Andore

"I want to love you madly. I don't want to fake it, I just want to make it…"
– Cake

W HILE LEAVING A GROCERY store, I was stuck behind an elderly couple plodding along with no haste. This may have been fast for them, but not fast enough for me. There was no way around them as they walked side by side, pushing a cart full of groceries. I was forced to slow down.

It was at that moment that I noticed something so small but so inspiring. A sample of their affection for each other was right in front of me, and I almost missed it. This sample was a glimpse of the mountain peak we have been discussing and are trying to reach in our marriages. The lady in front of me, walking tightly to her husband, had two fingers on her right hand lightly hooked on his back left pants pocket. Connecting them so slightly but signaling a bond between them. A bond that has probably overcome many obstacles during their long journey together. I bet those fingers represented a connection stronger than welded steel; a connection that bends and never breaks; a connection that may stretch but rebounds back. In front of me was a reminder of my goals for my marriage and my hope for yours.

I believe all the stats on marriage are missing one key area of study: Did the men go into marriage informed, intentional, and purposeful?

Having read this book, you are now informed and hopefully ready to be intentional and purposeful in your pursuit of the best marriage. Your marriage will have its tough times, but I'm confident you two will prevail.

Keep in mind that the woman you choose to marry will not be the *only* woman you marry. You will marry who she is today, but also the woman she is becoming and who she will be in the future. I've heard that those who make it on this journey *re-married* their spouse no less than three times. That is, they realized their spouse had changed and fell in love all over again. It's up to you to embrace her change, support it, and love her through it all.

I believe one of the greatest gifts in this life is our ability to choose. Reminding the woman we love that we choose her over all others is a gift we need to honor and remember. We need to know that this choice comes with a promise that we will be the men they need and that we will grow and change alongside them.

Change is a choice too. The man you are today is not the man you will need to be in order for this journey to be a success. The choices you make along the path of life and in your relationship will determine the outcomes.

I am not the man I was when I met my wife, and she is not the woman I married. We are both different versions of the person we committed to long ago. If you don't embrace the change, you will be one of the men saying, "we grew apart," a phrase that was probably preceded by your wife telling you, "You will never change."

Do not fear change; embrace it. Pursue it and be excited about what you will learn along the way. Be the Iron and Cotton for your wife and continually offer your strength and compassion through it all. Be an intentional and purposeful man in all that you do.

APPLYING IRON AND COTTON

- Write down at least three changes you plan to implement that were covered in this book.

- Iron sharpens Iron: What men can you ask to keep you accountable on your journey to be the best husband, father, and overall man? Talk to them within one week.

- Go tell your wife you love her and that you are ready to be that man she needs you to be. You got this! You have what it takes!

THANK YOU!

I have truly enjoyed writing this book for you. It was an unexpected journey for the past four years that I am grateful for. I've learned so much, and I am excited to share it all with you. I hope you now feel armed and better prepared. I pray you have an incredible marriage.

If you want some additional resources and want to continue the journey with me, please follow and learn more at: www.ironandcotton.org, #ironandcotton, search my podcast, "Iron and Cotton," and let's continue the conversation.

If you enjoyed this book, please spread the word, and together let's have a positive impact on marriage.

If you would be willing, I'd love a review. Reviewers can be a huge help to authors, and I genuinely want to know your feedback on this book. Thank you!

ACKNOWLEDGMENTS

God

My family and extended family

Josh Raab, my editor

Scribe Writing School

David Purdum

Zach Vail and all the people he introduced me to…first

Jason Sleeman

Mark Saunier

Ted Lowe

Peter Bourke

Dave Willis

Phil Adra

Curt Trotter

The Core 4 Couples

Ryan Lipe

Nick Hull

The Johnsons

All the men that did my survey

All the men that shared their stories with me

Laura Cotcher

No Longer Bound

Abba House

Northpoint Ministries and Browns Bridge Church

My Small Group of Men

My LDG Group of Men

John Eldredge for his book "*Wild at Heart*"

Timothy Wenger (The Man Effect)

Justin Bailey (Code of Character)

Mike Yarbrough (Wolf & Iron)

END NOTES

1   https://handkerchiefheroes.com/home/

2   Emotional Intelligence 2.0, TalentSmartEQ, authors Travis Bradberry and Jean Greaves, page 13

3   https://www.truphilos.com/feelings-wheel/

4   https://edis.ifas.ufl.edu/fy1274

5   https://www.health.harvard.edu/mental-health/can-relationships-boost-longevity-and-well-being

6   https://www.ncbi.nlm.nih.gov/pmc/articles/PMC3505409/

7   https://www.bustle.com/p/7-things-couples-therapists-wish-you-knew-about-healthy-fighting-vs-hurtful-fighting-8033031

8   https://www.psychologytoday.com/us/blog/conflict-matters/201802/the-benefits-arguing?amp

9   https://www.businessinsider.com/brene-browns-biggest-life-hack-is-a-simple-phrase-2015-8#:~:text=%22If%20I%20could%20give%20men,t%20be%20100%25%20accurate.%22

10 https://www.ncbi.nlm.nih.gov/pmc/articles/PMC3230928/

11 www.investopedia.com/how-to-avoid-financial-infidelity-in-your-relationship-4687135

12 http://press.careerbuilder.com/2017-08-24-Living-Paycheck-to-Paycheck-is-a-Way-of-Life-for-Majority-of-U-S-Workers-According-to-New-CareerBuilder-Survey)

13 https://www.nbcnews.com/better/business/keeping-joneses-can-help-your-financial-life-if-you-do-ncna858456

14 https://www.psychologytoday.com/us/blog/married-and-still-doing-it/201606/6-myths-about-pleasing-woman-in-bed

15 https://pubmed.ncbi.nlm.nih.gov/28678639/

16 https://www.songfacts.com/facts/marvin-gaye/sexual-healing

17 https://fightthenewdrug.org/how-porn-affects-the-brain-like-a-drug/

18 https://www.wakefieldresearch.com/blog/2017/05/10/new-wakefield-research-study-trump-effect-american-relationships

19 https://pubmed.ncbi.nlm.nih.gov/23745615/

20 https://www.liebertpub.com/doi/abs/10.1089/cpb.2008.0263

21 https://thepsychologist.bps.org.uk/volume-30/august-2017/forgiveness

22 https://www.aamft.org/Consumer_Updates/Infidelity.aspx

23 https://www.psychologytoday.com/us/basics/infidelity